SHAN
NEN
BADASS
DOHE
RTY

SHANNEN DOHERTY
BADASS

A HARD-EARNED GUIDE
TO LIVING LIFE WITH STYLE
AND (THE RIGHT) ATTITUDE

CLARKSON POTTER/PUBLISHERS
NEW YORK

All rights reserved.
Published in the United States by Clarkson Potter/Publishers, an
imprint of the Crown Publishing Group, a division of Random House, Inc.,
New York.
www.crownpublishing.com
www.clarksonpotter.com

CLARKSON POTTER is a trademark and POTTER with colophon is a
registered trademark of Random House, Inc.

Library of Congress Cataloging-in-Publication Data
is available upon request.

ISBN 978-0-307-59152-4

Printed in China

Design by Jennifer K. Beal Davis

Photography © copyright Shando Productions, Inc., except where noted below.
Pages 2, 3–4, 10, 12–13, 17, 53, 57, 64–65, 71, 82, 90, 97, 127, 150, 168,
201, 240, 251 © Kurt Iswarienko.
Page 31 cover photo by Andrew Eccles from *Rolling Stone*, February 20,
1992, © Rolling Stone LLC 1992. All Rights Reserved. Reprinted by permission.

10 9 8 7 6 5 4 3 2 1

First Edition

To my mom and dad, the two best parents a daughter could ever ask for. Thank you for your guidance, support, and endless love, and for always nurturing and believing in the badass in me even when I didn't. I love you.

LIVING BAD

MEANS NEV

TO SAY YOU

LIKE A

ASS

ER HAVING

ARE SORRY.

LIVING THE BADASS LIFESTYLE

From Makeup and Manicures to Motels and Movies

Welcome to My World

Difficult. Beautiful.
Self-destructive. Smart. Ugly.
Honest. Talented. Loyal.
These are just a few of the words people
have used to describe me. And these
words weren't just bandied about in local
coffee shops or bars. Having been an
actor for most of my life, I have spent a lot
of my time in the public eye. These words
could be found next to pictures of me in
magazines and newspapers, heard on talk
shows, and featured in entertainment
"news" and, sometimes, on the evening
news. Given my career choice and my age,
I have had plenty of time to go through a
whole range of experiences, with lots of
highs and lows.

Fortunately, my life experiences have taught me much about myself and about others, and about integrity, intelligence, religion, politics, honesty, and inner strength. One thing I know for sure is that labels are boring and often have actually nothing to do with the person; it is just the way others perceive you, or choose to perceive you.

Some people were motivated to perpetuate the name-calling because they were only invested in selling newspapers or getting higher television ratings. Did I deserve the negative labels? Well . . . um, yeah. But not all the time, and certainly not for the reasons they thought.

I hate when actors—or anyone who, like me, is fortunate enough to make a living at something as fantastic, mystical, and creative as acting—blame their job or childhood or fame for screwing them up. Sure, there are some occupational hazards, but I never hear these people complain about how they get the best tables in restaurants or tons of amazing clothes or any of the other fringe benefits of being a celebrity.

As for me, I am totally grateful to have been granted such an amazing way to make a living, and the lifestyle that goes along with it has afforded me more opportunities that I can count. The bottom line is that I wouldn't trade the hand I've been dealt for anything else under the sun. I also know that I wasn't always as gracious as I certainly should have been for the perks and pluses that came my way. But I've come a long way since those days. Hubris could have been my middle name back in that not-so-distant era.

What I don't like are "tell-all" books, because they are often untrue. In fact, if I was not an authentic badass I would name one right now. To me, they seem to be nothing more than a long list of excuses for how the person went wrong. How boring! Do people really care about their excuses for bad behavior? Really?

THIS IS NOT THAT BOOK!

BECOMING A BADASS HAS GIVEN
ME THE ABILITY TO BREAK FREE
OF MY INSECURITIES.

BECOMING A BADASS HAS GIVEN
ME THE CONFIDENCE TO LIVE MY
LIFE IN FULL AUTHENTICITY.

BECOMING A BADASS ALLOWS
ME TO BE COMPLETELY AND
ALWAYS TRUE TO MYSELF,
WHICH IS THE KEY TO BEING
ARTISTICALLY, EMOTIONALLY, AND
INTELLECTUALLY FREE.

BECOMING A BADASS MEANS
BECOMING THE BEST YOU CAN
BE. STRAIGHT UP AND STRAIGHT
AHEAD. STICK WITH ME AND
YOU'LL SEE.

More than ever, I love where I'm at now. I love the woman I have become.

Rather, my book is a guide that will tell you all about how I went from being a sometime bad girl, sometime confused girl, sometime angst-ridden girl to becoming a real badass. More than that, I hope it will be an inspiration. A motivation. A kick in the pants to gals everywhere to stop wasting their time and their talents because they don't have the self-confidence to step up to the plate and give the world their best shot.

Hopefully, by the time you are done reading this book, you will have all the confidence and assurance you need to feel good in your skin, live life with moxie and style, and enjoy all the benefits of living the badass way. Whether we're talking about dating, dealing with your frenemies, or having a completely amazing throw-down dinner party—you will do it with flair and guts, and have a ton of fun. I'll share some of my tips, but what I really hope you will take away is this: being a badass is the best thing you can do for yourself, your family, and your friends, because being a badass means you are being true to yourself.

The journey to becoming a real-life taking-names-and-kicking-ass kind of girl starts with having a warts-and-all moment with yourself. You've got to take a good hard look at who you are—**the good, the bad, and the ugly.** That was what I had to do to evolve, and that is what we'll cover in the first section of the book.

Once you know who you are—and because we all know you want to *become* a badass; that's why you're reading this book—we'll move on to the techniques for you to start putting your newfound badassness into action, especially where it counts the most: in **relationships.** In the second section of the book, I explore some of my past relationships to show you how to break out of negative behavior patterns by embracing the much more empowering behavior of the badass.

From there, the path of becoming a badass takes us out on the town and on vacation, and into living large, in general. The final section of the book—but by no means the end of the badass journey—is focused on the **essentials of the everyday badass life.** Having a badass attitude will affect everything you do, so that your confidence, style, and determination shine through in a bright—not bitchy—way.

I have to laugh at my old bad-girl image because, in all honesty, I'm one of the tamest human beings you'll ever meet—that is, unless you threaten to cause harm to me or to anyone or anything I love (be it man, plant, animal, or mineral). More than anything, I have learned to embrace, celebrate, and protect my core convictions and to be proud of what makes me tick, what makes me strong and sensitive and unique.

OPPOSITE: Being badass means getting the most out of life and having a blast.

READY TO BEGIN YOUR JOURNEY?

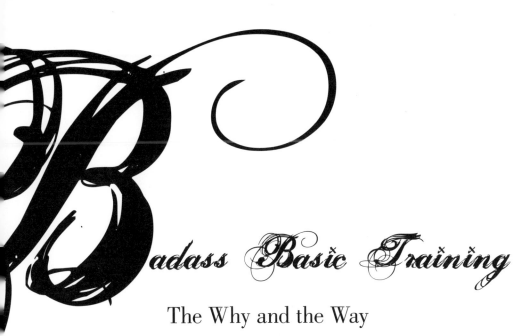

Badass Basic Training

The Why and the Way

What constitutes a badass? I look at this question and immediately think the opposite of what I know a lot of people may come up with. I don't think of *badass* as a nasty or derogative term for a mean-tempered, rough, take-no-prisoners kind of person, even though it is used in that way in different circles. But that's not how I see it. In the military, people associate *badass* with a person or group of soldiers who is tough and ready to do what's needed to get the job done. I think that is using the term *badass* in a positive way.

Similarly, I'm here to exalt the badass in all of us! I believe in being loyal and standing up for what you believe in, building family ties and strong friendships, appreciating the freedoms we have and loving the country we live in, and loving all that we've been given and fighting for what we believe to be right.

I have been in situations in my life that have been less than what I desired. However, armed with the love of my family and belief in myself, I have managed to maneuver my way down the good and bad roads in my life. I haven't always made the right decisions, but I have always been willing to deal with whatever came my way.

Before I dedicated myself to the badass way of life I was a mess of contradictions. I knew I was smart; I knew I was talented; I knew I had strong beliefs and philosophies. Despite all the good things and people I had in my life, I made a lot of wrong choices—especially when it came to my relationships with men, friends, and colleagues—mainly because I was afraid to really be myself. I found myself holding back and acting out to hide my laundry list of insecurities. I often kept the real Shannen under wraps until I finally decided, once and for all, to let the real me come out from the shadows.

I HAVEN'T ALWAYS MADE THE RIGHT DECISIONS . . .

I kept the real me under wraps in many ways, but the most significant way was in not showing my own vulnerability. I built a wall around me that was impossible to break through, in order to protect myself from feeling lost, scared, or any other emotion that was just too much for me to handle at that time. As for men, I chose them based on my belief that I could help them with their issues and

RIGHT: Being recognized and appreciated always feels nice, but a real badass knows she rules anyway.

BELOW: To have the privilege of leading the Pledge of Allegiance for the President of the United States at the Republican National Convention was one of the biggest honors of my life. A badass gets involved with the things she believes in.

THE PRESIDENT

August 26, 1992

Dear Shannen,

Thanks so much for leading the Pledge of Allegiance on Thursday night at the Convention. I really appreciate the time you took away from your busy schedule to be with us. You were a perfect representative of the new generation's voice in this election.

Barbara and I are grateful to have your support. With best wishes,

Sincerely,

their problems instead of focusing on my own. What was I thinking?

The day I decided to fully embrace my inner badass was the day the real me was finally set free. There wasn't one particular thing that made me embrace my inner badass; rather, it was a process of growing up and of coming to terms with myself. There are many moments that may lead you there—a failed marriage, a DUI, a job you won't be considered for because of your reputation. For every person it will be different; it's your own personal journey. The important thing is that you make the move and take the steps to becoming the best person you can be.

Getting there isn't easy, but boy, is it worth it. First of all, it means being true to yourself, dancing to the beat of your own drum. It's about being confident, courageous, cool, classy, and smart. It's the best blast you can have, and you can do it on a dime if you really try. All you need to learn is how to look at your life— past and present—with a different kind of eye. Find out what makes you happy and what makes you *you*. Then build on that— with conviction, integrity, brains, style, and a ton of moxie.

Women everywhere are striving to break out of their shells and live life to its fullest and most authentic potential. **We don't just want to have fun—we want to have a friggin' ball.** That's badass. Some of us may even want to (and will eventually) rule the world. That's badass. We are a breed apart. We have strong convictions and opinions and we wear them well—on our pretty sleeves or our sexy hems or our thigh-high boots or our favorite well-worn shoes.

OPPOSITE: Badasses can be hard workers, but we also know how to have fun. My friend Gary and I are caught goofing around on a break during a photo shoot for *Entertainment Weekly*. The shoot was for the show *Breaking Up with Shannen Doherty*.

Hello?

Are you tired of biting your tongue?

Are you tired of settling for second best?

Are you tired of sitting on the sidelines of life?

Guess What?

Badasses aren't.

I'm a badass and proud of it, especially of being a badass gal. Why? Because we rock. We roll. We have integrity above all other attributes. We have learned, often the hard way, from our own mistakes and experiences. We have taken that knowledge and put it to good use. We have used it to heal old hurts and to acquire new confidence. A badass is never a bitch, but a bitch can become a badass—if she really wants to and really tries.

Being a badass is fantastic. Who can say that better than I can? I've been the bad-girl bitch and the hermit and the people-pleaser enough to know that the badass life will now and forever be the life for me.

Being a badass is the only way for me to be . . . me.

Badasses have a
different way of
looking at the world.

POP QUIZ:
ARE YOU A BITCH OR A BADASS?

1. YOU CONSIDER YOURSELF COOL.

2. YOU DRESS FOR YOURSELF, NOT FOR OTHERS.

3. YOU DO AS YOU PLEASE.

4. YOU LOVE A GREAT REVENGE STORY.

5. YOU SPEAK UP FOR WHAT YOU BELIEVE IN.

6. YOU OFTEN ACT FIRST AND APOLOGIZE LATER.

7. YOU'RE A GREAT JUDGE OF CHARACTER.

ANSWERS

1. Toss-up. You could be either—bitch or badass.
2. Badass.
3. Bitch.
4. Bitch.
5. Toss-up.
6. Bitch.
7. Trick question! A badass never passes judgment on anyone, but is a great judge of character!

Bitch vs. Badass

Back in my Brenda Walsh days, when I was shooting *Beverly Hills, 90210*, I was definitely a major bad girl, but I never really thought of myself as being a bitch. I know that will probably make a lot of people howl, but it's true. To me, a bitch is a person who is intentionally malicious and manipulative, and I was never that. My intent was never to hurt another human being.

The truth of the matter is that I was screwed up. I wasn't facing my issues, and as a result, I acted out in all the wrong ways. I may have thought I was a badass, but I wasn't. It would be years before I could claim that title, before I could really own who I truly was, before I really *knew* who I truly was.

In my early twenties I was all about being emotionally distant, aloof. And I exercised very little self-control—that was one of my biggest issues. There was just so much happening. You know, I had been working since I was ten, and

ABOVE: Being a badass requires that you assert yourself, which can be bitchy or badass depending on your intention. It's like a machete, a tool that can be used to hurt a person or for something useful: I used this one to open a coconut at a friend's house in Mexico.

I sort of got out there on my own when I was eighteen, and the people I was attracting in my life were just not good for me. It wasn't healthy. It felt like there was absolutely no positive energy around me, and I just fell into all of that crap.

Those defense mechanisms of being distant and acting out were really my ways of coping with extremely deep-seated insecurities. First of all, the success of the show came on so strong and so fast that it was totally hard to believe. I mean, why me? I had no confidence at all back then, so I began acting like I did have tons of confidence. I walked around with a chip on my shoulder, as opposed to the real me. It was the only way I could figure out how to *be* at the time. I had yet to learn the hard lessons that go along with being an authentic badass.

Back then, I was scared . . .

That's how the defense mechanisms kicked in. I didn't realize it at the time, but I put on that bad-girl act to keep people at a distance because I was afraid—afraid of losing everything.

The persona that was put on my character, "Brenda," spilled over into my real life. So I became "Brenda the Bad Witch."

That façade hid my fear, but it also froze my heart. It kept my inner badass from seeing the light of day . . . until I finally took a good long look at myself and my life and decided that my time on this Earth is short. That's when I said, "Enough of this crap," and began living with full integrity. That's when I found the courage to really be me. That's when I made my mind up to become a badass.

OPPOSITE: Luke Perry, me, and Jason Priestley on the cover of *Rolling Stone*.

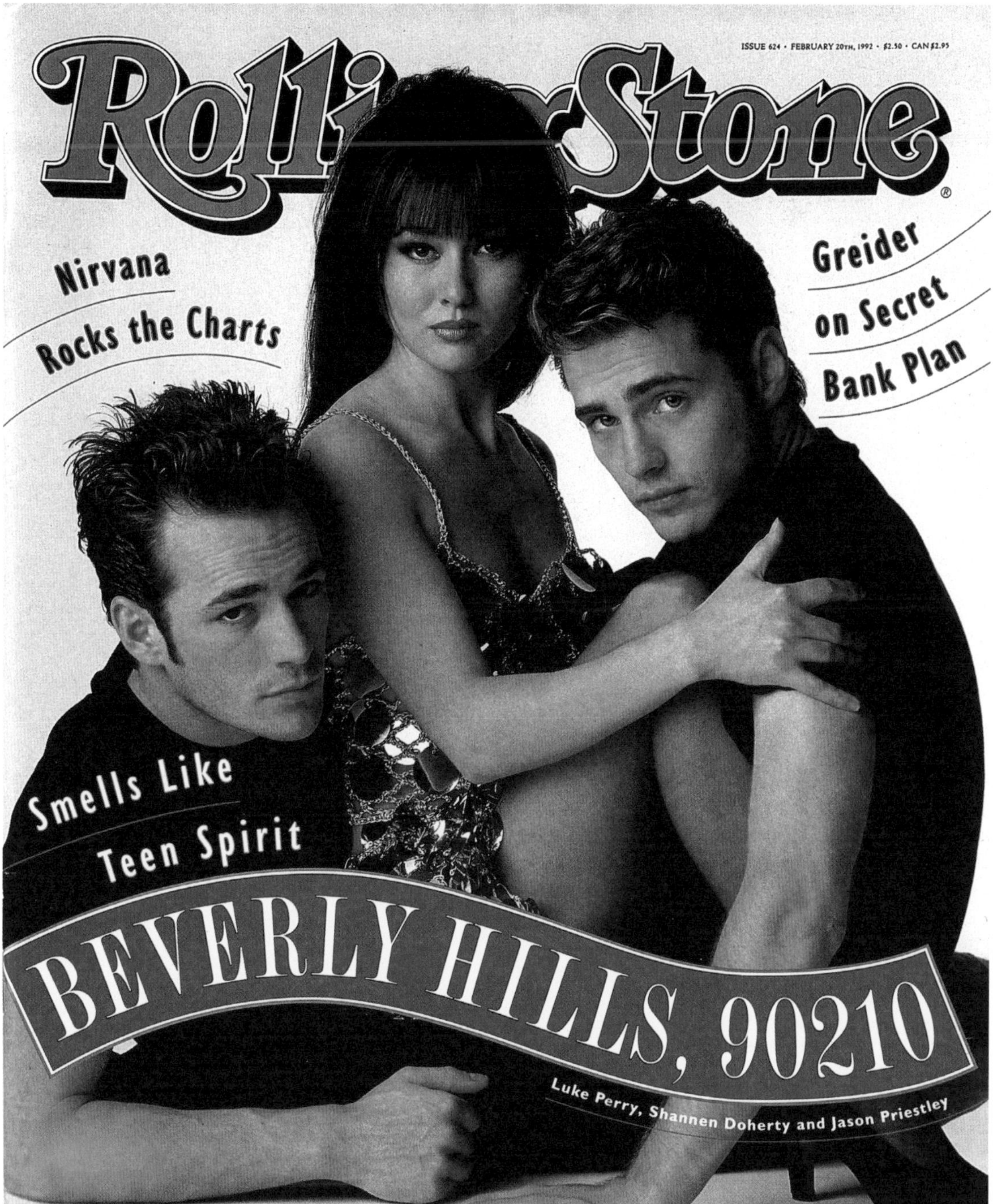

ISSUE 624 • FEBRUARY 20TH, 1992 • $2.50 • CAN $2.95

Rolling Stone

Nirvana
Rocks the Charts

Greider
on Secret
Bank Plan

Smells Like
Teen Spirit

BEVERLY HILLS, 90210

Luke Perry, Shannen Doherty and Jason Priestley

BITCH · BULLY · HERMIT · PEOPLE PLEASER · BULLSHIT ARTIST · BRAVE HEART · DEVIL MAY CARE · BADASS

Where Are You on the Badass Growth Chart?

Being a badass is a struggle; I don't think it comes naturally to everyone. A badass will fall down, have hiccups, make mistakes . . . However, a badass will always be able to see those mistakes sooner rather than later, and will correct them as well as stand up and own up to them.

Wouldn't it be wonderful if everyone accepted everyone else the way they really are? You know what? When you practice the fine art of being a badass, you'll find that people actually do accept you the way you really are. That's the payoff.

The tricky part is first learning exactly what a badass is versus what a badass isn't. Perhaps the toughest part of all is reviewing your own past behavior as well as your current personality traits in order to help determine where you fall on what I like to call "The Badass Growth Chart."

THE BITCH VS. THE BADASS

Bitches . . .

make the same mistakes all the time.

have no integrity.

have no class.

have no style.

have no sense of humor.

have no wit.

are not clever—just manipulative.

are always looking for an angle.

will walk over people to get ahead.

are tacky.

are bitchy, not bitchin'.

Badasses . . .

learn from their mistakes.

have integrity.

have class.

have style.

are smart.

are funny.

are witty.

are clever.

learn their lesson.

will work hard to get ahead, but never at the expense of others.

are flawed and know it.

are compassionate.

are loving.

are sensitive.

Choose Happiness

Life can be tough, filled with challenges and adversity. And there's no question that our experiences at a very early age help to shape and mold us into the adults we become. I listen to people blaming their childhood for why they do certain things, for why they are angry, for why they are victims. Of course, if you had a rough childhood, you have extra challenges in front of you, but it's up to you to overcome those challenges. Most people don't choose to be victims, but we *can* decide to be survivors and make the changes in our lives that are necessary to put the past behind us and move forward in a healthy way.

We all have our own individual relationship to happiness, and shaping that relationship is within our control.

Being happy doesn't happen overnight; it takes time, patience, and—most important—forgiveness.

A Baby Badass

My childhood was ideal in many ways. I had loving parents who raised me to believe in myself, gave me a strong moral belief

OPPOSITE: Circa 1978, Memphis. Determination is crucial to being a badass.

OVERLEAF, CLOCKWISE FROM ABOVE LEFT: My late grandfather was a man who loved badass women. My grandmother is a true badass. Circa 1973, my brother and I have always been close because we know how to enjoy our time. Circa 1978, from a young age, my parents encouraged me to be active mentally and physically. But all that activity can really exert a person; this is me circa 1980, napping on the set of *Father Murphy*. Circa 1975, even way back then I had a flair for acting. Circa 1981, the family who dresses in florals stays together. Circa 1977, badasses believe in all things. Circa 1977, two little badasses on their way to school.

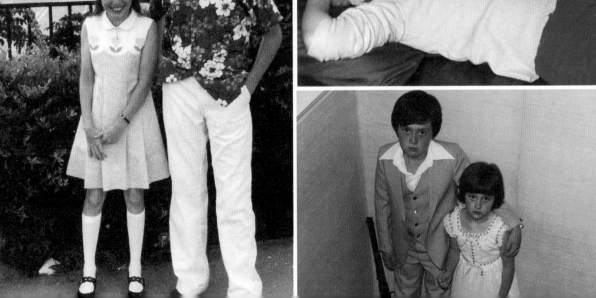

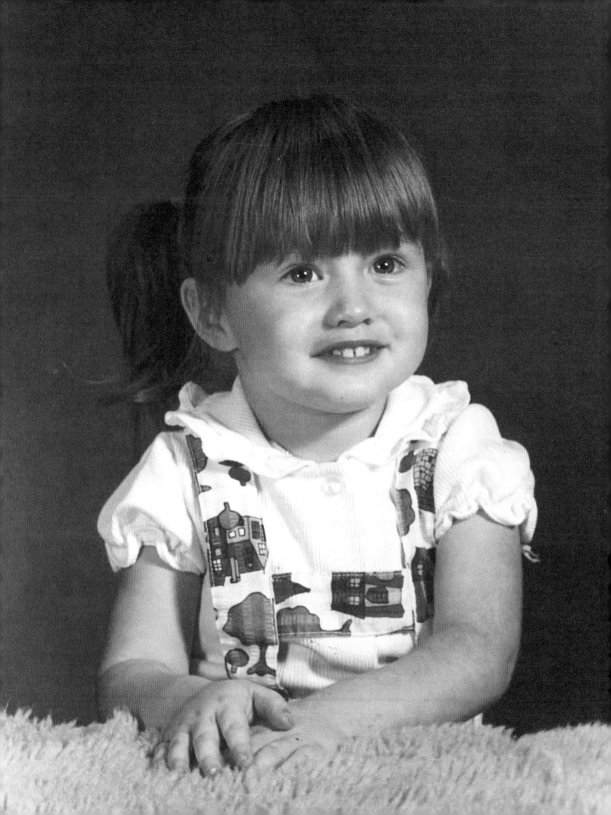

system, and supported me in all my endeavors. My sense of security was shattered, though, when my mom, Rosa, almost died when I was ten, and then my dad, Tom, got very sick. My father is my hero; I have always worshipped the ground he walks on. When he got sick, it rocked my world to the core.

Ever since I was twelve, we have struggled with my dad's health. Heart attacks, strokes, bypass heart surgery, kidney failure, he lost most of his eyesight and he has to fight to stay in this world. He worked and supported the family for as long as he could until it was just too much for him, and thankfully for all of us, by then I was making an okay living at this acting thing.

My mom, who is an amazingly strong woman, stepped in and got a job to help support us as well. At a certain point, I felt that my dad needed full-time care and I was scared for him to be left alone, so I asked my mom to quit her job to take on the new job of making sure my dad was okay. I have always been very proud that I was able to eventually step in and take care of my parents financially, allowing my mother, saint among angels, to take care of my dad, but I'll tell ya, it's a lot of pressure for an eighteen-year-old kid— and the feeling that I could lose my dad at any moment was a scary one.

Believe me, it took me years of therapy and soul-searching to really get in touch with those horrible feelings I had during my childhood. I kept all that stuff buried so deep inside that it was like going on an archaeological dig to finally bring those emotions to the surface so that I could take a look at how they affected me on so

OPPOSITE: Circa 1973

many levels as I was growing up. Now I realize that I was pretty much a walking bundle of nerves back then—not only so afraid of losing my beloved father and mother, but also carrying around the worry of what would happen to all of us if something were to happen to me. How would we survive? God, that was a lot of weight on my shoulders.

But I was a trouper. And a very good actor.

I walked around, unknowingly, with a fear of abandonment that I carried with me well into my twenties. By the time I was on *Beverly Hills, 90210*, I was working twelve hours every day and doing publicity on weekends, and my dad was not well. To say I had an attitude would be putting it mildly. But like I said before, I was scared. Scared shitless. I was scared that the one thing I loved doing, my escape, my passion, the job that allowed me the privilege of supporting my parents as they struggled with my dad's health, was just going to vanish. When you are so scared of something happening you can sometimes make it happen. It becomes a self-fulfilling prophecy. Diplomacy wasn't my forte back then, and I was too vocal about things that really could have just been left alone. Who cared if I thought an episode was stupid? Who cared what I thought of the script? It was my job to do my best with what was in front of me. I don't really know why I thought I had to voice my opinions so loudly. Was it to control something in my life when everything else seemed so out of my control? Maybe. Back then, I didn't know why I was angry, or why I was so scared all the time, but it all helped me to become the person I am today. What I do

OPPOSITE: Daddy's little girl grew up to be a badass.

know now is when to keep my mouth shut and be thankful for having a job doing what I love.

Darkness Before the Dawn

I have blown many opportunities that God has given me because of my fears, and I don't think that back then anyone actually knew what I was going through. I was very quiet about my dad and my responsibilities, as I didn't think it was anyone's business, and to be frank, I thought I was handling it fine, with a toughness that allowed me to work, support my family, and get through my days. It wasn't until I was around twenty-seven that I finally saw what I was doing to myself, to my parents, to my brother, and to my career.

I got a DUI when I was twenty-seven, and a good friend of mine, Adam Kaller, who is my attorney and has been in my life for more than thirteen years, looked at me and said, "Enough, Shannen! You are too kind, too sweet, too loving, and way too fucking smart for this. Get your shit together, *now*." I don't know why it was him who got through to me, because God knows how many times my own family had said the same thing, but for some reason Adam's words resonated deep inside of me, and I started on the path to healing.

My reputation has often overshadowed my talent, a talent God gave me and one that I cherish. I *love* acting—it is in my blood, coursing through my veins, and when I am on a set, I am alive and free. I love the collaborative process with talented directors, writers, producers, and actors. To crawl into a character's skin

OPPOSITE: My mother is a true badass and the person who taught me my first badass lessons.

and become that person is an amazing feeling, and I think I sold myself short by letting my personal life become the focus of what people see as opposed to my talent. During this time, I was letting my demons run the show instead of allowing my talents as an actress to shine.

It's not easy to look in the mirror and see who you have become and to know you have to change. It is painful and rough, and it forces you to face your fears and yourself. I had to accept my dad's health situation and find some positive way to look at it. To be honest, I struggle with that still.

I had to look at the choices I had made, from the men I chose to how I handled situations, to how I ultimately became self-destructive. As I said earlier, it requires time and patience and a brutal honesty with yourself. Of course, a shrink or trained therapist can sure come in handy because they can help guide you on your course of self-discovery. In my case, I found that God was the most helpful for me. But just know that turning to friends or close family members for help is nothing to be ashamed of. It's what people who love you are there for. It is definitely not a sign of weakness—quite the contrary.

OPPOSITE, CLOCKWISE FROM TOP LEFT: This badass always has a badass dog at her side, and Elfie went with me everywhere. Here we are on the set of *A Burning Passion: The Margaret Mitchell Story*, about the author of *Gone with the Wind*. Badasses-in-the-making come in all sorts of shapes and sizes. Before I could call myself a badass, I was all buckskins and buck teeth. Recognizing when special people come into your life is a crucial skill that a badass must hone. I was lucky to be able to work with Jack Elam on one of my first jobs, *Father Murphy*, which Michael Landon produced and lead to my next role. For *Little House: A New Beginning*, I played Jenny Wilder, and, much to my delight, I worked with the great Ralph Bellamy.

OVERLEAF: Another childhood delight was winning first place for a poem I wrote in the second grade. Even back then, I was creative and competitive.

To my darling Shannen ~ !xxo
Love and Kisses Jack Elam

"Walk on the Wildside"
1979 Poem Anthology

E.B & K.B. 79

* * * * * *

FIRST PLACE . . . . SECOND GRADE

<u>Walking On The Wild Side</u>

Walking on the wild side,
I see sand crabs crawling in the sand.
I see little fishes in the water
and sea shells lying on the beach.
I feel the water playing at my feet and
seaweed wrapping around my legs. I feel
the rocks under my feet and the wet sand
oozing between my toes.
When I'm at the beach
I feel God's presence as I
walk on the wild side!

                              Shannen Doherty, 7
                              Valmonte

* * * * * *

REACHING FOR HELP IS A SIGN OF STRENGTH.

Just the simple act of praying and letting my guard down while in that moment helped me reconnect with my softer side. Knowing that there was someone looking out for me helped me face the problems in my life and gave me the courage to change, to be strong.

I want to say this: a badass is a work in progress, always. We are not perfect, and we will make mistakes, but we won't make the same one twice.

I have made mistakes on my journey to becoming a badass, and will continue to do so, but it's the fact that I keep trying to better myself, that I never give up, that makes me a badass. I am always honest with myself, and I know I have so much more to learn.

I am not a victim anymore. I am a survivor— a fighter, in the right sense of the word. I look at life in a positive way and I no longer expect anyone else to swoop in and help me. I help myself. No one is to blame for my "terrible twenties" but me. Those days are behind me.

OPPOSITE: From my *Little House: A New Beginning* days.

ABOVE RIGHT: When I was six or seven, I idealized my brother, so I gave myself a haircut like his. Cute and brave, no?

THE BADASS

Here's the lesson: **STOP ACTING LIKE A VICTIM.** stop whining about your past, stop looking for handouts or someone to take care of you, and stop using your past as an excuse for your present. Get off your potentially badass ass and help yourself! It's not a man's job to rescue us or to take care of us, or our parents' jobs to figure out how to fix us. It's not the world's job to understand our pain because—believe me—the world has a lot more pain to deal with than any of us has.

It's our job as strong, capable women to help ourselves, to stand on our own two feet, and to support ourselves and be happy, content, and self-sufficient (not to mention self-efficient).

This doesn't mean I don't understand your fears, pain, and insecurities, because I do. I've been there. It just means that I am giving you a swift kick in the ass and using myself at my worst as an example of what you don't want to be and what you do want to become.

Your journey will be completely different. It will be your own. You may not have been a bad girl or a bitch in the past. You may have been more of a hermit, or a people-pleaser. But one thing we all have in common is our challenge when it comes to overcoming fear.

BOTTOM LINE

Fear of failure.

Fear of success.

Fear of abandonment.

Fear of ridicule.

**And the number one fear of all:
the fear of fear itself.**

The best-kept secret to being a successful badass is the ability to keep your fear in check. There's no such thing as "no fear." What keeps us on our badass path is our ability and desire to be fearless more often than not.

I took all the good things I was back then and kept them, and I threw away all the bad things.

Those times taught me who I never want to be again and keep me honest today.

I have raised my standards and reconnected with the original values my parents instilled in me, and every day I try my hardest to be a good person.

Now that you are beginning to understand the true nature and definition of what being a badass is, let's direct our attention to studying the finer attributes that make a woman a real badass.

Badasses We Have Known and Loved

Women have been forging ahead, using their inner badass strengths, forever. I had the opportunity to do a film based on the life of Margaret Mitchell, author of *Gone With the Wind*. Margaret was a fascinating woman who lived in the South in the early 1900s. She fought against stereotypes of what was expected of women of a certain upbringing and embraced her inner badass by going against the norm and taking a stand on what she believed in. As a result, she became a very successful woman despite having more than a few odds against her.

Amelia Earhart definitely had to embrace her inner badass in order to have the kind of courage it took to make the decisions she made as a female aviation pioneer. Although she was told over and over by those around her that she couldn't do it, she knew that she could and held on to her faith and belief in what she loved.

OPPOSITE: Being alone is not the same as being lonely.

Beauty can be found in the most unexpected places.

DOWNTOWN LOS ANGELES

TOP TO BOTTOM:
My best friend, Roger, and I will take off at the drop of a dime to check out a new scene. Here we are in San Francisco.

Long after the workday was done at *Charmed*, Holly Marie Combs and I stuck together, and she became a permanent fixture at my house. Here she is at one of the many barbecues.

My mom and dad always embraced my friends, just as my friends embraced my family.

Working with Shirley MacLaine (in a 2002 movie about the cosmetics mogul Mary Kay, who, by the way, is also a pretty great badass) was a wonderful experience for me. I see her as a true badass. Shirley is determined and successful in her work and has survived years in an industry that, even though it is making advances, has never been easy for women.

A badass can be the woman who works at the convenience store, the local salon, or the checkout counter at the market; she might be the CEO of a corporation, a restaurateur, a mogul, a movie star, a manicurist, a mom. A badass is anyone who is willing to stand up and do what it takes to get the job done.

In my book, a badass is also someone who works to live their life with complete integrity come hell or high water. And when it comes to being a female badass, the best thing about us is that we live life to the fullest while letting our brains, beauty, confidence, style, wit, and charm shine as bright as the fireworks on the Fourth of July.

RIGHT: Whether you are working twelve-hour days standing behind a cash register or sitting at a desk, a badass knows when to relax and enjoy the simplest things, like kicking off your flip-flops to run barefoot through the grass.

top 10 bAdaSSES

1. **Cleopatra** (69 B.C.–30 B.C.): Became Queen of Egypt at eighteen; mastered the art of love and war by leveraging her relationships with Julius Caesar and Marc Antony.

2. **Joan of Arc** (1412–1431): An uneducated peasant who helped the French defeat the English in the Hundred Years' War; was burned at the stake.

3. **Queen Elizabeth I** (1533–1603): Queen of England; during her reign there were great achievements in writing and there was peace in England.

4. **Deborah Sampson** (1760–1827): Fought in the Revolutionary War, pretending to be a man.

5. **Sojourner Truth** (1797–1883): African American who spoke out against slavery and for the rights of women.

from history

6. **Susan B. Anthony** (1820–1906): Formed the National Women's Suffrage Association; pioneer in the fight for women's rights; first woman to have her picture on an American coin (the silver dollar).

7. **Margaret Mead** (1901–1978): American anthropologist; famous for her study of how culture influences personality; lived in Samoa and studied the people there.

8. **Julia Child** (1912–2004): Revolutionized the way Americans think of cooking French food.

9. **Sandra Day O'Connor** (1930–): First woman to serve as associate justice on the U.S. Supreme Court.

10. **Diana, Princess of Wales** (1961–1997): Active in the fights against AIDS and land mines.

Great badass examples and inspirations are everywhere, not just in the history books. You'll find these supreme female beings in literature and music; on the silver screen, television, and the stage; in the streets, the boardrooms, and the bedrooms. The more you learn to spot 'em, the better chance you have of becoming one. I call this my "badass osmosis theory." Seek and thee shall find!

Top 10 Badasses from Popular Culture

1. Madonna
2. Angelina Jolie
3. Reese Witherspoon
4. Lucille Ball
5. Drew Barrymore

6. Sherry Lansing
7. Oprah Winfrey
8. Sandra Bullock
9. Katharine Hepburn
10. Tina Fey

The Basics of Becoming a Badass

Once you've determined where you fall on the Badass Growth Chart (see page 32), you can begin to navigate your way to full-fledged badassness by following a few of my tried-and-true rules.

When considering whom to include in my list of top badasses from popular culture, I was faced with having to be truly honest with myself about what it takes to deserve and earn that most enviable label. Remembering that all genuine badasses live their lives with full authenticity and integrity, I was torn about two famous females in particular: Lorena Bobbitt and Katharine Hepburn.

BOBBITT, you'll recall, became world famous in 1993 for slicing off the penis of her husband, John Wayne Bobbitt, after he reportedly came home drunk one night and forced her to have sex with him. Now, Lorena may have been feeling her full authentic rage when she did what she did, but I am troubled by her lack of full integrity when she followed through with that potentially fatal act of retaliation. Don't get me wrong, self-defense is definitely badass in my book. But revenge—especially borderline homicidal revenge—is not the way a badass woman rolls.

Verdict: NO.

Including HEPBURN, on the other hand, was an easier decision for me to make. Even though she should technically be disqualified as a bona fide badass due to her enormous lack of integrity in having a long-term affair with the very married (not to mention with children) actor Spencer Tracy, this iconic actress—I believe—should get a pass. While both Hepburn and Bobbitt exhibited a lack of integrity due to their own individual crimes of passion, Hepburn will forever live on as an inspiration to millions of badass women to come. Bobbitt will be lucky if her life makes the history books as a "girls gone wild" kind of footnote.

Verdict: YES.

Regardless of where you fall on that chart, keep in mind that all badasses-in-training must work their way through all of the rules, beginning at the beginning.

Rule Number One:

Badass gals live life with integrity at all times.

Having integrity is the key to all things badass. Integrity is a badass gal's calling card. It's her badge of honor, if you will. If you've known a genuine badass for any length of time, one thing you know for sure is that she can be trusted. You know she will always tell you the truth, that she will never steer you wrong. She means what she says, and her heart is in the right place. Having integrity is the main difference between being a badass and just being a bitch. That is why this is Rule Number One.

Speaking and acting with integrity will put you head and shoulders above the bitches and bad girls, who will be remembered only for their boldness or their shamelessness. When it comes to teaching you how to become the best badass you can be, I can only use my own experience and evolution as an example. People who knew me years ago, before I embarked on my own personal trans-formation into badassdom, might have pegged me as a self-centered bitch. I can understand that conclusion, mostly because of the way I often acted, but it's not really correct.

What helped me to anchor my true spirit and to begin on my path toward badassness was taking a good hard look at myself, at how I treated others, how I expressed myself, and how I was living my life. The first thing I found—which is something that I actually always knew—was that I may have acted out in some very unladylike ways, but I always had a core of integrity in my soul, a core that I decided to grab on to and build on.

You need to know what you believe in and what you stand for. I'm not here to tell you what is right or wrong or whether sleeping with someone on the first date is good or bad. That's for you to decide. But once you decide, you've got to make that your story and stick to it. You've got to have integrity, a philosophy, and a set of rules to live by.

Badasses always live by the golden rule: Do unto others as you would have them do unto you. For me, the golden rule is the underlying premise of integrity because it keeps you honest and on the path of your own moral compass. The idea of karma is another way of looking at the golden rule and maintaining integrity: **What goes around comes around.** But this doesn't give you license to be a total bitch just because someone wronged you in your life. Instead, it means you should treat others with the grace and openness with which you would want them to treat you. A badass handles everything with integrity, compassion (and passion), and a great deal of grace.

ABOVE: On the set of *Charmed,* celebrating my birthday. The crew was fantastic and made me feel loved.

BADASSES
AREN'T BORN . . .

THEY BECOME.

Integrity can come down to little things, like being on time. If you say you're going to meet someone at seven, be there at seven, or a few minutes earlier, but not later. Don't be a flake. You've always got to be honest. If the guy at the gas station gives you a twenty-dollar bill instead of the fiver you are owed in change, give it back; don't be greedy. The philosophy goes all the way up to big things like leaving a marriage when you realize you are no longer in love with your partner, or quitting a lucrative job when you lose respect for your employer or the product you are pushing. Stop living a lie.

Integrity means standing firm for what you believe in. Mind you, I'm not talking about a little bit of integrity here and there. I'm talking about major integrity—major integrity, all the time.

Rule Number Two:

Becoming a badass means facing the truth about yourself.

I admit it. I was screwed up. I was a bad girl back in the day because I wasn't facing my issues. I was a good person, but the fear of losing what I loved most in the world created negative patterns in my behavior and led to poor choices at work and at play. I wasn't dealing with the problems in my life. You know, I was running from the fear of losing my father, of losing my mother. Fear of losing them both was a constant stress during my childhood, and I think that kind of deep-seated anxiety can really alter a person. It can alter you in a bad way, or it can alter you in a good way.

In my early twenties, it definitely altered me in a very bad way.

My journey toward becoming an authentic badass began when I

decided to take a good look at myself. I looked at what I had done, how I had behaved, what I wished I could change. This is something that you must also do.

The easiest way to start is by making a list. Write down as many of your unbadass traits as you can. (Go back and look at the list of badass traits on page 31 if you need help remembering what is badass and what is bitchy.) Making this list was important for me, and it's important that you do it, too. It's the only way you can move forward toward becoming the best badass woman you can be.

ABOVE: My dad took this picture of me when I was six years old. It was my first outing to the beach, which has become one of my favorite places to be.

Being what I call "emotionally distant" was at the top of my list. Close behind was "having little self-control." That was actually the real issue for me. A badass knows how to set boundaries— remember what I said about integrity. A badass knows her limits and the limits of others. By writing up my list of undesirable traits, I was able to first own and then examine my behaviors in order to learn how to improve upon them. **Self-awareness is key to self-improvement.**

In order to live like a badass—with integrity—I needed to see where I went wrong so that I could right it. In my case, my lack of self-control seemed to stem from simply too much, too soon, and

ABOVE: When you have parents like I do, you are bound to embrace your inner badass at some point. They taught me everything I ever needed to know about love, respect, integrity, and the importance of family.

from my fear of losing my father and being totally abandoned. Looking closely at your fears will help you to unleash the strength and confidence you need to become your true badass self. Once you know what your issues are, you can work on tossing out the bad behavior in favor of the badass behavior.

I was so scared of losing people in my life that I started pushing them away. Friends, family, coworkers, you name it. I pushed them away however I could, either by shutting them out or by being a bitch to them. It was definitely a defense mechanism for me, a way for me to hold on to some kind of control. It was my way of leaving them before they could leave me.

Looking back, I now know that I acted out because I thought I didn't deserve all the success that had seemingly fallen into my lap with the success of *Beverly Hills, 90120*. That was a bitter pill to swallow, but it got me to where I am today—a happy, centered, confident person. Speaking of confidence . . .

Rule Number Three:

Becoming a badass takes a lot of confidence.

Self-esteem is a wonderful thing. Like integrity, it brings out the best in us. Like soul-searching, it centers us and makes us feel what it really means to finally embrace what is true. Having a healthy amount of self-esteem is probably the trickiest of the three rules. Gaining and maintaining a strong sense of self-confidence is the badass gal's greatest secret to personal and professional success. It will help balance your actions and reactions.

I know from my own experience that being an authentic badass means being a work in progress. To this day, even after a healthy amount of therapy, I still struggle with the issue of confidence. The difference now is that I know it's my weak spot. I don't need to obsess about it anymore. It's nothing but negative energy that is *not* authentic. It's not true. It's not badass. It's not me.

I don't need to pinpoint it anymore because I certainly think I deserve success now. Knowing that allows me to live with integrity. Believing that allows me to be my true badass self.

Connecting with the confidence that every single baby on this planet is born with is essential to becoming a badass. Have you ever watched a baby crawl around and explore the world? They're totally unreserved and lack self-consciousness. They're not thinking, *Oh, no, I can't wear this onesie because it makes me look fat.* They're just out there, with their boundless energy, determined to figure out how this fascinating world works. Finding out the reasons why you may be lacking in the self-esteem department is imperative if you are to succeed in your quest to becoming a powerful and happy badass woman. That's why you need to be totally honest with yourself—remember Rule Number Two.

In my case, I know that in my twenties I didn't think I deserved anything I was given because my self-confidence was shot. And when you feel like you don't deserve something, you try to destroy it. Privately and publicly, I was in a pretty self-destructive mode. Definitely not badass material. No self-reflection. No self-confidence.

The only way your confidence can shine is when you give it half a chance. So if you want to be a badass, you've got to work on

OPPOSITE: This is me when I was styling and art directing a photo shoot for a magazine. I loved being behind the camera and determining the look and feel of the shoot. Having confidence in a job well done is instrumental to being a badass.

golden rule..............

Integrity

1. If you are going to commit to something, follow through. No more flaking out or half-assed efforts.

2. Be on time for everything. The only exception is when you're dating. (See page 125.)

3. If someone slights you, take the high road. Know that it's not your job to teach them a lesson.

4. You should give people the benefit of the doubt, but that doesn't mean you should be a sucker.

5. Don't keep your mouth shut when you witness wrongdoing, unless speaking up would get you or someone near or dear to you seriously injured or killed.

The Truth About You

1. Look back on any situations you have regrets about and imagine yourself as the other person.

2. Follow your intuition. Learn to trust yourself. Be sensitive to what your gut is telling you.

3. If you don't like something, just accept that fact about yourself. Say you really hate eating sushi, but all of your friends always want to get sushi. Just say no. Suggest something else. Don't just go and be resentful about eating tofu again.

dos & Don'ts

4. Don't beat yourself up. You may have been there and you may have done that—whatever terrible theres and thats they may have been—but today is today. Get on with your life and move on. Start becoming the best badass woman you can be.

Confidence

1. Every day when you look in the mirror, find the things you like about yourself and think about them for a moment. Appreciate all the amazing things about yourself.

2. Once you start learning to trust your intuition, you'll find that you are right about many things. This will help build your confidence.

3. Accept compliments instead of waving them off with an "Oh, it's really no big deal" kind of remark. Learn to say thank you and to smile when someone goes out of their way to say something nice or positive to you.

4. Don't hide your light under a barrel. If it helps to spur you on, keep a daily journal where you document all the great things you do each day.

conquering those negative thoughts. **Badass gals always see the positive in every situation.** It's what makes them shine. It's what gives them an edge and a leg up. It's what makes them the best.

Now, don't get me wrong. It's not like a badass is a Pollyanna—far from it. It's just that when the times get tough, the genuine badass gets busy looking for potential opportunities in the situation.

She's So Badass!

Now that you're on the road to becoming the best badass you can be, I'd like to give you some reinforcing realities of how your life will begin to change—for the better.

The first thing that will happen is that you will start to believe in yourself. By living with integrity, in full truth and awareness of yourself, and with your negative thoughts kept at bay, you will begin feeling better about just about everything that you are and do.

In no time, you'll find yourself becoming much more decisive about what you like and don't like, from fashion to politics to your social life and working environment to the vehicle you drive.

Choices will begin to open up to you more than ever before. Possibilities will now seem reachable. Your voice will begin being heard—maybe not loud, but certainly clear.

Badass gals are a power to be reckoned with. They are a force of nature. They are divine.

A Badass

Always . . .	Never . . .
tells the truth.	uses the word *can't*.
maintains her integrity.	walks over someone to get ahead.
behaves like a lady.	comes off as stupid.
looks to improve herself.	disrespects her parents.
educates herself.	is malicious.
respects others.	counts on someone else to take care of her.
respects herself.	
keeps a positive attitude.	

There's More to It Than Just Following the Golden Rules

Being a real badass gal is great, but it's not always a piece of cake. It takes work to be the best you can be. Like I said earlier, being a badass means being a work in progress.

Believes . . .	Is . . .
in herself.	strong.
in others.	confident.
in doing good.	stylish in her own unique way.
in setting a good example.	
in forgiving.	beautiful inside.
in love, in whatever form that is.	fallible.
	smart.
in hard work.	funny.
in perseverance.	interesting.

In addition to being true to herself, an authentic badass gal has a lot of tricks up her sexy sleeve. It's not just about being authentic and confident. It's about having an edge. Or, rather, *the* edge.

Badass gals always make sure they are at the top of their game. That's how they maintain their confidence. That's how they are able to live their life with full integrity.

Badass gals *own* their badass attitudes, whether they are heavy or thin, tall or short, old or young. They make their badass brilliance *work* for them. They make no apologies for who they are or what they believe or what they wear or how they behave.

You either accept them or you don't. They couldn't care less, because they know that if you don't "get" them, you probably never will. So they move on. They keep on keeping on because they know there is nothing to gain by forcing an issue, friendship, or what have you.

Every badass gal's motto is "Life is too short to fuck around."

Skills are necessary to be a genuine badass gal, and one of the most important is to be an awesome observer. Paying attention to everything is a hallmark of a good badass gal. She makes it her business to study the people who are part of her world, be it in the home or the workplace, on the dance floor, at the bus stop, or in the bank or the bakery. Wherever there are things to be learned, she is learning.

PAYING ATTENTION TO EVERYTHING IS THE HALLMARK OF A GOOD BADASS GAL

In Summary

The path to being a badass isn't an easy one, and it requires quite a lot of soul-searching and honesty. You have to be willing to look at yourself and admit to your own faults, to how you hold yourself back and why. I feel that this is the most important part of being a badass, because until you truly reach deep down inside yourself and take a cold hard look at the dirty, ugly side of yourself, you can't really find the beauty that is there, the confidence, the talent, the humor, the smarts and wit.

I basically chose to not work for two years, accepting only jobs that were necessary to pay bills so that I could turn myself inside out and examine everything I had done, all of my bad habits, my patterns, my self-destructiveness . . . all of it. Let me tell you, it was scary for a while there, and lonely as well. It was just me, by myself, facing my demons, facing myself, and ultimately I had these huge moments where I was just like, *Oh my God, what an ass I was* or *I can't believe I did that* or *Why the hell did I allow that to happen?* Those moments can really take you down, but I believe from my own personal experience that they can also bring you way up, allowing you to find the room to improve and find better forms of yourself and others. I did this with myself, asking those hard, painful questions, like, *Why can't I find peace? Why can't I achieve my goals? Why do I have so much conflict in my life? Why can't I find a good guy?* Eventually, the answers came to me.

I know not everyone can push the pause button on their life for two years to get their badass credentials in order, but what you *can* do is simplify your life by cutting out as much bullshit as possible. Quit the drama and soap-opera crap. The second and third sections of this book will go into more detail about how to do that, but really, the point is, you need to start with yourself and make *you* a priority in your life.

When I took the time to stop focusing externally, I discovered why I couldn't find peace—I wasn't at peace with myself. I was constantly at war with myself, trying to be perfect for others, trying to hold it all together, yet inside I was a mess. Here I was, leading this very adult life, dealing with business every single day, but internally I was a scared child. I couldn't achieve my goals because I was literally standing in the way of myself. I was making enemies at work and feeling like I didn't deserve my own success, and therefore destroying all good things that came to me.

Conflict? Well, when you aren't at peace and happy with yourself, you aren't going to be happy with others, which leads to finding good men and friends. You attract what you put out, and if I was trouble, that's what I was going to attract. I faced all of this and kept going within myself to get to the root of my issues, my insecurity, my destructiveness, all of it. I stared my bad shit down, and guess what—I WON! I now control my own destiny, I'm a peaceful person, and I have a confidence that isn't shaken simply because someone rejects me on the Internet or in a newspaper. I believe in me, and I truly like myself.

Most important, I forgive myself for the mistakes I made—yet I will never forget them. Being a badass requires this deep soul-searching and is something we all owe ourselves because we are women, and we are strong and capable and beautiful. Let's own that in life, because if we do, there is nothing we can't achieve!

ABOVE: My dad and me at Donegal Point in Ireland. This man is my heart and soul.

The Badass 10 Commandments

1. Thou shalt live life to the fullest.

2. Thou shalt be true to thine own self.

3. Thou shalt never hide thy light, brains, or brawn under a bushel.

4. Thou shalt be clever.

5. Thou shalt have style.

6. Thou shalt pay attention.

7. Thou shalt trust thy gut.

8. Thou shalt always strive for excellence.

9. Thou shalt be confident.

10. Thou shalt be cool.

The Badass Art of Love and War

Family, Friends, Lovers, and Professional Relationships

How many times have you told yourself, *Next time will be different* when it comes to romance, a job, a friendship disaster, a disagreement, a family gathering, or simply your average everyday situation where you want things to go your way?

Plenty, you say? Me, too, back before I decided to become the best badass I could be. Time after time, I found myself falling into the same old traps and patterns. I always landed right back exactly where

I was the last time I traveled down a familiar path when it came to the way I handled (and frequently mishandled) my relationships.

SO, IF YOU'RE SICK OF ALWAYS ENDING UP WITH THE PROVERBIAL SHORT END OF THE STICK WHEN IT COMES TO THE GAME OF LOVE, LIFE, AND THE PURSUIT OF HAPPINESS,

WELCOME TO THE CLUB.

Lord knows you're not alone. Every badass gal I have ever known has been there and done that. In most cases, more than once.

Some call it looping—that banging-your-head-against-the-wall-until-you-can't-see-straight kind of repetitive negative behavior. I call it like it is—crazy. But crazy is as crazy does, and I've been victim of that silent enemy more times than I can count, until I finally decided to do something about it by going badass on it all when it came to having healthy relationships with family, friends, lovers, and coworkers.

After nearly a lifetime of either keeping my head buried in the sand or unsuccessfully throwing my weight around when it came to trying to get what I wanted in any given situation, I finally discovered the real secret of success when it came to dealing with relationships, both personal and professional. One of the first steps to having good relationships with others is to have an awesome one with the most important person in your life: YOU. Remember the three rules outlined in the first section? Here's a quick refresher:

1. Have integrity.

2. Know yourself.

3. Have self-confidence—then you can begin to deal with
others in a positive way. If you follow these rules you'll be more able to accept others for who they are, and therefore more able to choose your friends and your fights wisely. Badasses know when to stay and fight and when to leave and say, "Forget it; it's not worth it." We can pick and choose our friends and our fights. We can take or leave what comes our way or make a dark day bright just by turning on our inner light. In hard times we can ride out the storm. When the time is right, we can soar to our heart's delight.

The one thing all genuine badasses have in common is that they have all learned to take full responsibility for their actions. And by that, I mean we have learned to own up to the things we have done right in the past and, more important, to take responsibility for the things we have done wrong.

That was the biggest step I took when I decided to leave my bad-girl, or "difficult," days behind. (For others that might mean

BADASS GAL'S GUIDELINES FOR A GOOD RELATIONSHIP

- BE TRUE TO YOURSELF.

- BE HONEST AT ALL TIMES.

- KNOW WHO YOU ARE.

- KNOW WHAT YOU LIKE.

- KNOW WHAT YOU WANT.

- KNOW WHAT YOU NEED.

- KNOW WHAT HASN'T WORKED IN THE PAST.

- KNOW WHEN IT STOPS BEING FUN.

- KNOW WHEN YOU TRY TO CONTROL OR CHANGE OTHERS.

- KNOW WHEN IT IS TIME TO CUT AND RUN.

shedding their people-pleaser or shrinking-violet personas.) Taking a good and honest look at the way I acted in previous relationships, both on and off the set, was crucial in order for me to even consider becoming the awesome badass woman I knew I was born to be.

What I learned when I looked in my rearview mirror was that in the years before my twenty-seventh birthday, I was very, very hard. You know, when I finally got totally honest with myself, I realized that I was so hard back then that there was just no getting close to me—not on the job, not in my personal relationships with my parents, family, and friends, not with my boyfriends. I don't think I was ever really close to anyone.

Taking a hard look at our past behavior doesn't mean we have to beat ourselves up. Just the opposite. One of the hallmarks of a true badass is her natural ability to be soft when she needs to be. And when it comes to identifying and reviewing the mistakes of your past, you need to be plenty soft on yourself. In fact, that softness is part of the process of becoming a badass.

To Thine Own Self Be True

I sent an email to somebody the other day, and in it I wrote, "You know, I can totally back off, but then I'm not being true to myself." I've always been an all-or-nothing kind of gal, and it's pretty much always brought me success. But when I say "always," I mean since I was twenty-seven.

That's how I know this stuff works.

It's the difference between knowing who you really are and connecting to that person. Being soft with her. Being forgiving of her. Instead of running away from the pain of a situation, or turning away from turmoil or grief or fear, we need to learn to embrace it.

I let my former lack of self-esteem take over who I really was. And it took me almost ten years—from my age of dawning enlightenment at twenty-seven—to figure out that the person I was pretending to be was *so not me,* and my behavior wasn't making me happy. I was miserable within because I didn't know who I was.

ABOVE: With Tim Bitici on the mean streets of New York City. He's a badass friend and damn good stylist! You just can't go wrong with a gay man who knows how to dress you.

It boiled down to this one basic badass gal mantra: To thine own self be true.

Pure and simple (yeah, hardly), this mantra is a badass gal's secret weapon. Because once you really know who you are, and are sensitive to your own needs, you will know what your limits are. When I didn't know what my triggers were, I just reacted blindly. Now that I have a sense of where my weak spots are, I know what I can and can't handle. And because I've got boundaries and am more in tune with my senses, I'm better able to telegraph more positive vibes. Once you know your limits, you'll start attracting like-minded people, people who respect you and your integrity. It's called synchronicity.

I'm not talking about the "my way or the highway" school of behavior when I profess the magic powers of embracing the "to thine own self be true" school of thought. Just because I know what I want doesn't mean I'm a total dictator about things. Badasses get the job done with our brains, not our brawn or our bitchiness. A genuine badass does not have to resort to being a bully or a bull-dozer in order to get her way when it comes to winning friends and influencing people.

What it really boils down to is much more subtle and sophisti-cated in nature.

Welcome to my "master class" in being a real badass.

Take notes.

Enjoy the ride.

Lose Control

When I looked back on all of my failed relationships, the boy-friends who didn't work out, the marriages that broke down, the people on set I couldn't work with, they all had the same thing in common: at one point or another, I tried to control them. This isn't to say that they didn't need to be controlled. It's just that I didn't need to be the one to try and get them under control. Because at that point, it became a huge negative for me!

For me, that was the "bad pattern" I needed to break before I could be the successful badass woman I knew I could and should be when it came to the relationships in my life. As I was learning, the more confident I felt, and the more courageous I became—and the more courageous I became, the less I found myself want-ing and trying to control everything, and everyone, around me.

Seriously. Back in the day, before I earned the right to call myself a B.A., I was a control freak. Not that I don't still have some control issues—I know that much about myself. Being a badass certainly does not mean you are perfect. But you can't make the relationships work alone.

Truth be told, I still want to control my personal relationships. That will always be part of me. But what I've learned since becom-ing a B.A. is that it's not about "them" when it comes to whether the relationship is good—it's about me.

When I feel that urge to control a relationship coming on, I now see it for what it is—a sign, a red flag, a warning that I am slipping back into negative old behavior patterns that have never worked out well for me. When those warning flags show up, they are the equivalent of a blinking stoplight.

Stop, Shannen. Something is not right here. What's wrong with this picture? What's wrong with this relationship?

The answer is that it's not healthy for me, and it's not working for me. Rather than going down the old road of the way I used to behave, trying to "fix" it all by controlling people, I try instead to keep the focus on controlling myself. I now realize that when I find myself repeatedly wanting to control someone or something, it is a definite sign and message that this relationship or situation is not healthy or good for me. It's a sign for me to use my confidence and my courage to move on.

CONFIDENCE WILL GIVE YOU THE COURAGE TO GIVE UP TRYING TO CONTROL WHAT YOU CANNOT CONTROL.

The minute you stop trying to control the actions of others in a relationship, you automatically gain the upper hand. You'll also be much better at breaking unsuccessful old behavior patterns because you'll be much better at knowing when to stay and when to cut and run. This also applies to relationships on the work front, with your friends, and even, for some, with family members.

Charm

Another trait that badasses have is charm. Charm is either a God-given gift or a learned talent, but whichever way you slice it, a

OPPOSITE: Holly Marie Combs and I loved getting dressed up on the set of *Charmed*.

girl has to have charm! Charm will get you out of a lot of messes and will endear you to people. Now, when I say charm I don't mean that superficial crap of just smiling and batting your lashes at someone. I'm talking about having manners, humility, personality, and confidence. We have all seen that person who can light up a room with a smile, whose energy is infectious and makes us feel good, who commands attention without seeking it out, who can make others feel important and special.

There are those who possess the natural abitlity to walk into a room and instantly be noticed, not because they are beautiful or well known, or for any obvious reason other than they are just charming. They are charming because they are interesting and comfortable with themselves, and they somehow leave you with a

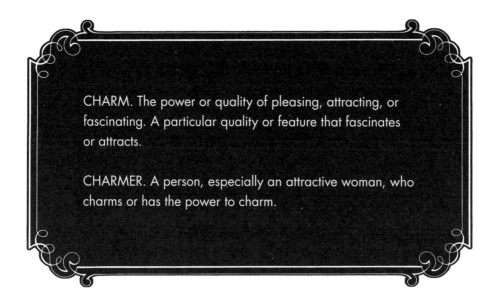

CHARM. The power or quality of pleasing, attracting, or fascinating. A particular quality or feature that fascinates or attracts.

CHARMER. A person, especially an attractive woman, who charms or has the power to charm.

good feeling about having met them and been around them. A woman with charm knows how to listen to others and make them feel special just by how closely interested she is in them.

The power of pleasing, attracting, or fascinating (charm) is knowing what to do in various situations, and when. There is a strength that can be gained by walking into a room, introducing yourself, and finding out about the people you are meeting. Extending your hand with a broad smile on your face and introducing yourself to someone demonstrates confidence and attracts interest from the other person.

Southern women have always been known for their ability to charm those around them. It's as if the quality of charm is bestowed on them at birth and built by the guidance from their loving families as they are allowed to develop all aspects of their character. Respect for others is taught from a young age and, more important, so is respect for oneself.

A Southern woman is attractive and fascinating due to the dichotomy of her very being, that being the "steel magnolia" factor. As gentle, subtle, and pleasant as she can be, the Southern woman is also known for being strong in the face of adversity and situations that call for a special strength. That special strength is tucked away but easily accesible to her if she needs it.

Staying Positive

We all have moments when life seems to be beating us down, dealing us one bad card after the other. It's during these times that you must reach deep down and pull out all the badass attitude you have to keep your head up and your back straight, and to walk with pride, confidence, and a smile. There will be obstacles on your course to being a badass, but it's how you deal with those obstacles that is important. Look, no one knows better than me that there are haters out there trying to drag you down. The person at your office who likes to make you look bad, the so-called friends who make snide comments about you, the guy who gets nasty after you turn him down, the catty girls who just don't get you—we all know those people. But how does a badass deal with them?

A very long time ago when this whole Internet blogging thing started, I used to read what people thought of me and have painful reactions. I had many a moment when I cried because someone I

didn't even know was putting down my looks or my acting. They assumed that they knew what I was all about and drew harsh conclusions about me. I was devastated that anyone out there could feel such hate for me that they would actually post about it. It often tore me down and took me days to forget what they had said.

ABOVE: Badasses always look up.

ABOVE: Sometimes things aren't always perfectly in focus.

The negativity would seep into my brain and affect the very core of me. One day, I was crying to a friend about it and she said to me, "Shannen, have you ever met the people who make those comments, have you ever looked them up and seen who they are, what they do? Could you ever imagine doing that? NO and that's because YOU have a life!" With those words, I realized that the majority of people who put others down are simply sad, insecure, and bored with themselves. These are people I should never give any thought to. My friend helped me by telling me to remove myself from their negativity. Instead, I took a hard look at the people who were making the comments and came to my own conclusions about them. I mean, how do they have the time to post unless they have very little going on for themselves? What kind of

ABOVE: I have known the fabulous Laurent and his charming wife Fabienne since I was twenty.

Reputations

Reputations—everyone has one. Some are good, some are bad, some make you smile with pride, and others make you sneer with anger. My rep is questionable at best, and something I have struggled with since my tragic twenties. The thing about a reputation is that once you get one, it is nearly impossible to change. No one understands that you were just going through an "experimental" phase, an "angry" phase, a "slutty" phase, or just plain old teenage angst. A bad reputation sticks like industrial glue and is the first thing to walk through the door. I have had my fair share of moments where I have sat at home crying my heart out over an unfair judgment of me due to a rep I acquired when I was troubled, sad, confused, and messed up. I continue to ask the question "Why can't people forgive the mistakes of my youth and see me for me?"

Well, welcome to having a REP!

There are ways to change your rep, of course. Adopting a baby from another country is a good one. You can start delving into some heavy charity work; become a recluse, therefore earning the new rep of "freak"; write a tell-all book blaming your childhood for everything; start delivering cookies to your neighbors for no reason at all; hire a "spin doctor" after showing up in a sex tape; cry publicly about the starving children in Africa; go to India on a soul-searching trip and find God. All of these will give you a solid shot at changing your rep, but how will you feel about yourself? Yes, we all care about how others perceive us—even me—but what I find most important in my life is that I can look in the mirror and be proud of myself. I have never fought rumors about myself, instead opting to take the high road and just stay silent. My thought was that whoever was lying about me would have bad karma and eventually be revealed for the manipulative lying piece of shit they are (yeah, no anger here . . .) and I would remain unscathed and classy. Um, right, so that didn't work out too well for me, but I continue to just keep my head down and try to be good a person.

Okay, I know there are lots of holes in this thinking. If I'd listened to my brother, who is a male badass, I would have fought the lies and rumors as if I were at war, with an amazing strategy, and endurance.

SUCCESS IS THE GREATEST REVENGE.

person gets joy from someone else's pain unless they are trying to mask their own? It made me feel sorry for them and for the people who start these gossip blogs. Can't these people make a living creating something with their own talents, minds, and hands as opposed to making it off of others' success (or off of their failure for that matter)? What did these people do prior to blogging? How did they earn a living? Do they contribute anything positive to the world, or is it all just negative crap they put out there? All I can say is that karma is a bitch. We live in a world where the Internet has allowed us full access to everything and everyone, and sometimes that's good, but a lot of the time it's bad. No one deserves to be picked apart, scrutinized, put down, and allowed no privacy to live their life their own way, mistakes and all.

Here's the lesson for you baby badasses: ignore the ignorant, ignore the negativity, and, if anything, feel compassion for the haters because that is all they can do with their lives. It is definitely not badass to be a negative blogger or to tear others down. **DON'T PAY ATTENTION TO PEOPLE WHO ARE TRYING TO DRAG YOU DOWN.**

Don't pay attention to people who are trying to drag you down.

What is badass is to stay positive, give people the benefit of the doubt, and focus on your own life. I have learned this lesson over many years and now refuse to read about myself or give these people an ounce of my time. I stay positive and I like myself—for those who don't like me . . . too bad for you!

Family First

Anyone who knows me knows that I adore my family. They mean the world to me, and I am nothing without the love of my father, mother, and brother, Sean. This isn't to say that we don't have our disagreements and bad moments, or that my love for my family doesn't cause me grief at times. In fact, my strong attachment to my family and my fear of losing my parents were the underlying causes of all that internal stress during my childhood, which led to my fear of abandonment and major insecurities and issues—and you know what that led to.

Just as important as knowing yourself is knowing where you come from. And coming to terms with your family situation is key. I'm not going to say that you need to have a picture-perfect relationship with your parents or have amazing ties to family like I do, but to really shine as a badass, you've got to come to terms with your relationship with your family. Because let's face it: our upbringing and our parents shape us in ways that are pretty fundamental to how we see the world. Our heritage is part and parcel of who we are as people. And our first relationships in this world are with our parents. I'm no psychologist, but it seems pretty clear to me that understanding how we deal with our parents is important to understanding how we relate to others in the world.

That's why family is first when it comes to looking at the relationships in your life. I'm not saying you should put your family above all other relationships, but knowing where you come from

OPPOSITE: Quality time with my family runs the gamut from decorating the Christmas tree to helping my father dig a pool in our backyard.

and understanding how you feel about your family is important to having good relationships with your friends, boyfriends, and colleagues. If you've got a great relationship with your family, like I do, then embrace it, celebrate it, let your parents and siblings know you care about them.

If your relationship with your family is not so stellar, then recognize that, too. Accept and forgive yourself, and your family and the people who have wronged you; this is going to help you tap into your badass side. Remember, badasses own up to their mistakes, have the confidence to see life and others for what they are, and don't try to control people or situations.

FAMILY IS FIRST WHEN IT COMES TO LOOKING AT RELATIONSHIPS IN YOUR LIFE.

So what can you do if, say, your sister married the most annoying person on Earth or your cousin's husband tells the same terribly tasteless joke every holiday? Nothing. That's right, I said nothing. These people are not your problem, and you're better off keeping your piehole shut if it means you get to enjoy your time with your siblings and family. Remember, a badass knows which fights to pick, and these are not the battles to fall on your sword for. Of course, if there's something seriously wrong and you see someone taking advantage of or abusing someone you love, you've got to stand up and fight, but for petty annoyances, just let it go. Badasses take the high road.

OPPOSITE, CLOCKWISE FROM TOP LEFT: My brother, Sean, is smart, strong, and loving. Sometimes badass is in the genes . . . my grandparents were two of the original badasses. My parents: you can see the love between them.

Badasses and Children

In my opinion, there is nothing better than a badass having a kid. We need more badasses in this world, and if a child comes from one, chances are the child will be a badass, too. A badass parent is a sight to see, and I know them intimately, having been lucky enough to come from two badasses myself.

My parents raised me to think for myself, to have strong opinions, and to stay true to my morals and convictions. Watching TV wasn't really a part of my childhood. Instead, my parents sat my brother and me down with books and the newspaper. We were required to read up on current events and discuss them over dinner. Our reading list growing up was more challenging than that at most schools, and as a result we were well-spoken and smart.

My dad raised me to believe that I am equal to any man, taught me how to defend myself, and instructed me to count on my brain rather than my looks. My mom raised me with a very strong belief in God and guidance on right and wrong, and taught to be myself regardless of how different that may be. From her I learned to embrace who I am and never conform or change for others.

Raising children is as much an art form as it is a test of a person's ability to see the ultimate project of life through to its fruition. Children are the true legacy of the badass. There is no better way to share the spoils of the badass life lived to its fullest than to inject the circle of life with a round or two of badass children.

OPPOSITE: Spending quality time with my goddaughter, Cooper, rates high on my list of favorites.

Think about it: In the end, why are we all here as human beings? Survival of the fittest? Maybe. That evolved us out of the animal kingdom, but we humans are the only species on Earth with an innate ability to reason. Believe this badass when she tells you that our ability to reason is no small thing. It's a unique and powerful gift we humans have, and it is in fact what separates us from being mere animals . . . that and the opposable-thumb thing we have going for us.

ABOVE: My parents have always encouraged me to do anything, including racing BMX bikes.

CONVO WITH THE KIDS

I have seven nieces and nephews and a goddaughter, and I can tell you that they are exceptional because of how they are treated. My brother, Sean, and his wife, Thanne, are two of the smartest people on Earth, and they treat their kids with utter respect. They have always encouraged them to form their own opinions and talk about what is going on in the world. Sean and Thanne educate their kids in every way, and as a result they have kids who are very secure, smart, and self-assured.

My nieces and nephews have been going to restaurants since they were born, and now that they're from elementary to high school ages, they're expected to sit at the table and participate in the conversation.

I was on vacation recently, and sitting next to me at a restaurant were two kids with their parents. The kids were watching a movie on a portable DVD player with earphones plugged in while they were eating. Okay, thank you for using headphones and therefore not subjecting the rest of us to *Finding Nemo,* but come on. How hard is it to engage your children in a conversation at dinner or expect them to sit there and behave themselves while out dining? What kind of world do we live in where parenting has become sticking in a movie or a video game and plopping your kid in front of it? Furthermore, what kind of future is this world looking at with them being the next generation to have a voice on what happens? *Talk* to your kid, your niece, your nephew, your friend's kid. Talk to them, and help them learn the skills they will need to survive and flourish in this world—because I honestly don't think *Grand Theft Auto* is going to help them.

So, it stands to reason that procreation is certainly more than just perpetuation of our species. To the badass, procreation is the ultimate incarnation of our life's work. It's the five-course meal prepared by a five-star chef and served hot at the world's dining table to not only provide sustenance and nutrition, but to do so with refinement and style and a discerning eye for quality, well-executed process, and thoughtful integration of techniques acquired over a lifetime's devotion to learning one's craft and practicing it with pride and perfection.

In other words, having kids is an exquisite opportunity to show the world everything a badass is about.

Friends and (Fr)Enemies

Badass gals make some of the best friends in the world. Why? Because we so thoroughly know who we are that we can pretty much always give the best of what we've got to those we love.

You can't be a badass if you can't create and maintain strong, healthy, and happy relationships. It's called balance. It's called wholeness. You can't be a badass gal in every aspect of your life, but when it comes to forming strong emotional bonds with other like-minded people, you're the best. You can't have a successful professional life and a personal life that is in shambles. It just won't work. At least not for long.

BADASS GALS MAKE SOME OF THE BEST FRIENDS IN THE WORLD.

OPPOSITE: This is my Great Uncle Stan. I adored him, and he made me feel special every second of the day.

Remember: being a badass woman is about excelling, about pushing yourself to be the best human being you can be. So if you find yourself winning at the game of life, but you're lonely, you know you need to do more work on yourself—and to make time and room in your life for being with friends.

An authentic badass woman does not need to have a hundred people around the table at her birthday party. A badass doesn't need to be the most popular person on the planet. But a badass *should* have excellent friends, even though there may be only three or four of them around at any given time. It's about quality over quantity. And there are few things better than real, true, genuine friends. An authentic badass girlfriend will never let you down (if she can help it).

The tricky part for us badass women is that our sheer brilliance often sparks competition, and sometimes downright contempt, from those who are not badass enough themselves to not feel threatened by our charms.

The rub also comes when you are not being authentic in your personal life. If you have an old pal who does not subscribe to the badass ethic, you need to distance yourself from that person. If you send a gentle message that you no longer tolerate inauthenticity or a lack of respect or integrity, you will begin to generate a new, much more badass group of friends.

And since badasses are not judgmental, you'll soon be attracting a much more fascinating and diverse group of pals. Now, more than ever, you will be open to people of integrity that you may never even have noticed before. And vice versa.

HOW TO WIN FRIENDS
AND INFLUENCE PEOPLE
THE BADASS WAY

1. WORK AND PLAY NICE
   WITH OTHERS.

2. SHOW CURIOSITY ABOUT THOSE WHOM
   YOU WANT TO WOO.

3. SINCERE FLATTERY WILL GET
   YOU EVERYWHERE.

4. MEAN WHAT YOU SAY AND SAY WHAT
   YOU MEAN.

5. BE DIRECT.

6. KNOW YOUR SHIT.

7. BE TRUTHFUL.

8. BE CANDID.

9. BE HONEST.

10. BE CONFIDENT.

LOYALTY

My best friends and lovers have all had one thing in common: loyalty. It's simple: if you are not loyal to me or to my family you'll never get any tea, sympathy, or love from me. Betrayal is the biggest deal-breaker for a badass. No two ways about it.

Loyal friends would never:

- Gossip about or team up against one another.

- Date—or even flirt with—their friend's ex.

- Share a secret they promised they would keep.

- Speak disparagingly about one another or one another's family members (including pets).

- Ignore you when you are in need.

- Compete to be the queen bee or top badass.

In short, your social circle will expand. Badass class acts attract, fascinate, and encourage one another!

A Badass Girlfriend Is a Friend Indeed

She is a great listener.

She is a great source of inspiration.

She can always cheer you up when you are down.

She can always point you in the best direction she knows.

She will always tell you the truth.

She is fun.

She knows you inside and out.

She accepts you for who you are.

She's your cheerleader.

She's your shrink.

She's your stylist.

She's your sister.

A Word of Warning

One thing B.A.s need to be constantly on the lookout for are what I call "cling-ons," those poor weaker souls who always seem to gravitate toward the light, which in our case is us. Badass gals burn bright, so we are easy targets.

We're also known for our kindness (not to mention coolness), so we need to be on guard. Why? Because cling-ons pull you down. They sap your energy and drain your strength. They come in all varieties—male, female, friend, colleague, family member, total stranger, hidden foe.

Imagine that you're a bird, and you're flying along, and then somebody totally lassoes you and ties you to the ground. You're

flapping your friggin' wings, but you can't fly because they've got that rope holding you down. That's what cling-ons do to you—they just ultimately hold you back from being yourself.

You'll know a cling-on when you see one. They are needy. They are starstruck. They are overly helpful. They are irritatingly self-conscious. They are outrageously ineffectual. They rarely, if ever, express an opinion. They live in a state of constant dread. Where cling-ons go, drama follows!

The B.A.'s Art of War

As with everything badass, when it comes to dealing with conflict, it's all about being true to yourself, being prepared and self-assured and willing to learn from your mistakes. There's only one hard-and-fast rule we follow when we're going into or find ourselves already in the middle of battle: we never, under any circumstances, let the enemy see us sweat.

If you're in the middle of an argument and you are at a loss for words, you can always disarm the other party and give yourself more time to dream up the right comeback or decision by saying to them, "You know what? I'd like to research that a little bit. So let me get back to you on that."

I use this technique all the time. I keep a Post-it next to my phone that reads: "Research!" Whenever I get stuck for an answer, this always buys me a little time, thus giving me the advantage.

PRECEDING PAGES: Badasses drive with the top down.

OPPOSITE, TOP: Roger and I have been best friends since I was eighteen years old.

OPPOSITE, BOTTOM: Birds of a feather flock together. Roxana is a badass girl who has an awesome handbag line called One October.

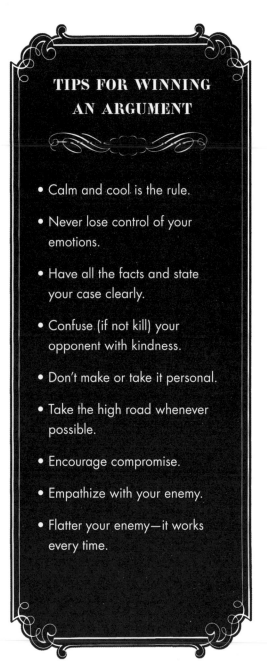

TIPS FOR WINNING AN ARGUMENT

- Calm and cool is the rule.

- Never lose control of your emotions.

- Have all the facts and state your case clearly.

- Confuse (if not kill) your opponent with kindness.

- Don't make or take it personal.

- Take the high road whenever possible.

- Encourage compromise.

- Empathize with your enemy.

- Flatter your enemy—it works every time.

Learning as much as you can about your enemy is also a must for every badass gal before she goes into battle. Know your enemy's strengths and weaknesses. Do your homework. Be prepared. Stay strong. Remain confident. Visualize success.

On Revenge

Badass women have much more important things to focus on than plotting and seeking revenge. Success, for a badass, is the best revenge.

When someone screws us over, our mode of operation is best summed up as "moving on." I mean, really, who has time for that bullshit? Even better, we view that sorry excuse for a human being as being dead. They are "dead" to me. They are "dead" to us. Poof! Bam! Whoosh! That person simply ceases to exist.

They become "dead" because they are too inconsequential for us to even think about. Gone. "Who? What? Why, I have absolutely no idea who you might be referring to!" They are much too insignificant for us to waste our precious time on.

Revenge? Who needs revenge? Fuck with me once, it was my mistake. Fuck with me twice, and you're dead. You're dead in my mind. And a mind is a terrible thing to waste. **A badass may forgive, but she will never, ever forget**. Got it? Good.

When to Weed Out a Friend

A bad friend, or "frenemy"—you know, those friends/enemies who pretend to be your friends but treat you worse than your meanest enemy would—can be like Kryptonite to Superman. If you start feeling used by a friend it will always end up tampering with your confidence, and when that happens, it is time to let go of that friend. If you have a friend who is always asking for your advice about the same guy or the same job or the same anything but doesn't show signs of following your suggestions—or of reciprocating when you need her shoulder to lean on—then you've got to cut that chick loose. If you don't, she will end up sapping your energy and zapping your strength.

IF YOU WANT TO BE FRIENDS WITH A BADASS, YOU'VE GOT TO AT LEAST SHOW SOME EVIDENCE THAT YOU ASPIRE TO BE ONE YOURSELF.

If you want to be friends with a badass, you've got to at least show some evidence that you aspire to be one yourself.

Boyfriends and Lovers

Not every badass woman needs or wants to have a love of her life by her side. In fact, that's a choice many of us end up making after we do the work of really getting in touch with who we truly are and what it is that will make us happy. Commitment is not for everybody; perhaps this is even more true for the female badass. Her confidence and self-esteem are so strong that she is perfectly happy flying solo. But that does not mean that she does not have successful relationships. Far from it.

I wasted a lot of time in my twenties. Not that I didn't have great times and great loves. But it was still wasted time. Why? Because I didn't know myself well enough to know what was good for me. I wasn't badass enough to know better.

COMMITMENT IS NOT FOR EVERYBODY; PERHAPS THIS IS EVEN MORE TRUE FOR THE FEMALE BADASS.

I won't burden you with the details of my two relatively brief and tabloid-worthy marriages—the first to Ashley Hamilton (George and Alana Hamilton's son), and the second to Rick Soloman (who, after we split, went on to become legendary for unleashing the Paris Hilton sex tapes on the world). When it comes to Rick, I'm not going to lie and say I didn't love him. I did love him. And he provided a lot of great things for me during our relationship, especially humor. He was great at making me laugh, and we had some good times. But, my God, they sure didn't equal the bad times.

If I had been as badass then as I am now, I would have seen the warning signs. I would have had enough confidence, courage, and

ABOVE: Bowling, like life, can be a team sport. Or not.

clarity to see that there was a lack of integrity and morality going on in both of those marriages.

I blamed myself for being so blind. After my second marriage I sunk into a deep pit of despair. I kept thinking, *Okay, what was all that therapy for? How could I have been so stupid? Why do I keep choosing the wrong guys?* What I should have been saying to myself was *Okay, so you made a mistake. Learn from it and move on!*

That's what a badass gal would say, and she would end up being a lot smarter and stronger for it.

Badass Gals Give It Up!

Remember that part in the *Sex and the City* movie when Miranda talks about her husband cheating on her? She didn't understand why, but they hadn't had sex in forever. My friend had this same conversation with me about her relationship: "He has strayed; he cheated on me; he seems to have lost interest." I then found out that she hadn't given it up to him in months! Granted, there is no good reason or excuse for cheating—and it is usually an indication that there is a much larger issue in the relationship than lack of sex— but why hold out on your man? I am of the mind that if your man is satisfied at home, he will not stray.

Of course, there are just some flat-out scumbags out there, and if you have one of those you should leave . . . fast! But sex is essential in a romantic relationship. It makes men feel empowered, masculine, and virile, and when we withhold we are taking that away from them. I know, some of you are thinking that I live in a very old-fashioned world with that mentality, but there is something to be

1. Dispense with the notion that men are laboratory animals and dogs, even though they are.

2. Test them. Be frumpy—go without wearing makeup. Be late. Make them drive through the worst traffic to get to an event that you miss because you forgot the address or left your iPhone at home.

3. Surround yourself with people who make you happy. Fill your free time with activities that you enjoy.

By following these badass suggestions, you will inevitably attract a partner worthy of your supreme badass being. Not everyone is qualified, so use these three techniques to weed out the wanna-bees. Why do these techniques work?

Number one shows you being open and nonjudgmental. It's important to take things at face value and not have too many preconceived notions. Number two finds you being authentic (in the extreme, just to stress the point). Number three has you following your passion, which shows that you know how to have a great time and are a blast to be around.

Believe me, if you practice all three tips, you'll find yourself with a great mate in no time. Who wouldn't want to be in love with a badass like that?

said about blending the new with the old. I am a forward-thinking woman who has her own career, her own opinions, and her own money.

I stand up for myself and am self-sufficient; however, I am also a lady, and I believe in letting a man be a man. I take care of my man very well. I cook for him, I massage his scalp, and, believe me, he has no reason to ever stray. I refuse to cut him off at the balls by saying no every night. I know there are times when you just can't, but my point is you shouldn't get lazy in a relationship. Don't get complacent and take your partner for granted.

I BELIEVE IN LETTING A MAN BE A MAN.

We as women are very vocal about our needs, whatever they are. Men are not as vocal. They keep things to themselves a bit more, but trust me, they don't like going two days without sex—much less weeks.

Abstinence is also a choice, and a badass makes her decision based on what feels right for her. If this is the right choice for you—stand firm.

Oh My God! What the Hell Are They Thinking?

It's inevitable—we all get comfortable in relationships, but there is such a thing as "too comfortable." I am astounded when women I know start complaining to me about their relationships, saying that their man doesn't find them sexy anymore, their sex life is nonexistent, and the passion has waned. As I talk with them about why and how it is usually revealed to me that they don't bother to shave their legs anymore, their underarms look like King Kong's, and their, um . . . other area is a forest that no man could ever even find! Then they talk about how they like certain aspects of being comfortable, like peeing in front of their man and even—gasp!—doing the dirty number two with the bathroom door open.

OH MY GOD! What the hell are they thinking? No passion? DUH! Ladies, please stop this immediately! First off, how hard is it to shave your legs and arm-pits? Is it really just too much to go to the waxer once a month? And how hard is it to shut the bathroom door?

Let me put it to you this way: if your boyfriend or husband casually sat on your face and let out the smelliest, loudest fart in the world, and then just got up as if it had never happened, and he did this regularly, would you still find him hot? No, you would not. So why on Earth would he find you sexy when he can see and hear your bathroom habits? Now, I am clearly not an advocate of wearing makeup to bed or waking

RIGHT: At photo shoots, I like to tap into all different kinds of emotions to get different looks.

up early to "put on your face" so you always look perfect, but why should he have sandpaper scraping his body all night in bed? Why should he wonder how he ended up with a gorilla instead of the beautiful woman he fell in love with? Why has he ended up with a roommate as opposed to someone who lights his fire? There is no excuse for not taking care of yourself. It doesn't take much time, and grooming is important to us all. I feel it is important to keep some mystery in the relationship, some intrigue, and it takes work to keep the passion alive—but it is well worth it.

My grandmother, Southern belle that she is, has a rule about not leaving the house after five without heels and her face on. This may be outdated to a certain extent, but the basic idea is still good. We should put some effort into our appearance, we should shut the bathroom door, we should keep our hair clean and shiny and our body in good condition, etc. You do this not only for your guy, but for yourself. Have pride in your appearance, respect yourself, and put forth the best you that you can at all times.

Pick Your Battles

We are all guilty of forgetting this one. We focus on everything our guy isn't doing and stop acknowledging the good. WTF? I'm going to get dangerous here and possibly offend any man who actually was brave enough to pick up this book and read it, but here goes . . . When you are training your dog, you praise him as much as you scold him—hopefully more. How are men different? They aren't. They want you to recognize the effort they've made regardless of how big or small; you need to pat them on the head, so to speak, and give them praise and love.

If every time he does something good you simply move on and focus on what he *hasn't* done, you will get a man who stops doing anything that takes effort. I am the same way. If I have made a huge effort and my man just lets it go right by him and instead focuses on something I did wrong, I only get resentful and stop putting forth as much of an effort. You see, it's all about balance. Pick your moments to complain; don't do it the minute he walks in the door from a hard day, and don't do it when he brought you flowers to end an argument. And thank him for *his* effort, recognizing it and showering love and support on him for getting it.

ABOVE: Men, like dogs, respond well to praise. Give your man lots of it.

Dough Boys & Other

While most truly badass women have fantastic radar when it comes to finding an appropriate mate, some young up-and-comers need to sharpen their B.A. skills a little more in the patience department before they take that next big leap into the sea of love.

Practicing the art of watchful waiting is something I know I've had to focus on in my lifelong pursuit of a soul mate. As B.A.s in training are often prone to do, I've been known to be a little too optimistic in the past when it comes to the chances that a new romance will work out. None of us is perfect, but when it comes to finding the perfect mate, let's just say that some are more ready than others. I've got a great friend who came up with a phrase that helps me keep my head together when I find myself falling a little too fast in a new romance.

She was dating a lot a while back, really making the scene, which I thought was totally great. Instead of sitting around waiting for the real thing to come along, she decided to hit the singles' scene with a vengeance. Great gal pal that I am, I loved hearing all the juicy details about the various guys she was going out with.

After she worked the field for a while, I thought she had finally found someone special. They'd been going out pretty steadily for a couple of months when all of a sudden I found out that she was back on the dating scene. "So, what was wrong with that one?" I asked as I

Half-Baked Ideas

poured her a nice glass of red wine when she came over to my place so we could catch up and watch a movie.

"Him?" she said. "He was too doughy."

"What?"

She continued, "He's got to go back in the oven. He's not done baking yet."

I loved it.

You know, it's like sometimes when you bake a batch of cookies and you love the smell and you look inside the oven and they look all brown and bubbly and wonderful and you reach in to try to sneak just one—and the one you pick is still doughy. The problem with dating Dough Boys is that we tend to think we can put them back in the oven to bake a little longer.

I used to be like that. But now that I'm a badass, I say, "Screw that shit." It is not our job to cook these guys. Or to cook our friends, for that matter. Lesson learned: If a romantic partner is half-baked in the whole-person department, don't waste your time. Move on.

Ease Up on That Leash!

We all have control issues, but come on, ease up! There are women out there who control where, as a couple, they eat; what movies they see; what programs they watch on TV; what he wears; and his hobbies. They even complain about that hand of his that seems to rest oh-so-comfortably down his pants. Don't make these things the battleground of the relationship. Instead, try to compromise and be understanding, and, yes, even give in to his whims sometimes. Let him pick a restaurant, and when he does, don't roll your eyes as you say okay and don't sit there throughout dinner acting miserable with his choice. A sports bar can be fun, and isn't it nice to see him in his element?

Men don't want to see only romantic comedies. They want action or mystery, and is it going to kill you to sit in a dark theater holding his hand while he enjoys his choice, considering he does it for you all the time? *America's Next Top Model, Grey's Anatomy.* Okay, I get it, I love those shows, too, but give up control of the remote! Let him watch football sometimes, or the History Channel, Discovery, or the Food Network—whatever tickles his fancy.

Again, this is where balance comes into a partnership. It's give and take. We all want our guy to look good, but even we love slob days for ourselves where we just lounge about in our sweats, so let him be HIM. It doesn't mean you can't give him a helping hand in the wardrobe department, but there is no need to be consumed with it all the time.

As for the hand . . . you all know what I'm talking about—he is watching TV and that hand just seems to be permanently glued to his, um, manly parts. Well, let him! If he is in public doing this, that's just gross, but the hand down the pants around the house while watching TV is a freebie for any man, so just relax and let him do his thing.

Badass Babes Know the Real Thing When They See (and Feel) It

For me, the biggest indicator that a match is truly made in heaven is when the people in the relationship complement each other. They're not identical clones of each other, more like a teeter to the other's totter. Badass couples don't need to want to do all the same things all the time or have all the same interests, but there should be a balance of good stuff. If he's into music, for example, they may go out to watch bands on Friday night, to balance out the gallery crawl she organized with her arty friends for Saturday. On Sunday, they'll have "me" time, alone. I don't think love (or even friendship, for that matter) is about sacrificing who you are for the other human being. It's about finding somebody who shares your major purpose, which for a badass woman is always all about striving to be the best human being she can be.

In my case, I have found that I attract both the strong and the weak when it comes to men. I think I've attracted some really strong guys who could stand up to me, weren't intimidated by me, and were pretty much perfect for me. But I've also attracted really weak men. Maybe I sold myself short at the time, and went out with them because I was thinking, *Oh, I've got to help this person.* That was one of the biggest lessons I needed to learn on my way toward becoming a true-blue badass. I needed to stop trying to help people. Instead, I needed to work on helping or fixing myself.

IN BETWEEN RELATIONSHIPS, SPEND SOME TIME SOLO TO REGROUP.

Now that I am a much more whole person, I can really see that when I look back on my past relationships. I know from my own experiences that every time I allowed a weak person into my life, the minute they sensed any weakness in me—bam! They grabbed hold and started tearing me down.

I'm not saying that badass women are never emotionally vulnerable. Because, in truth, I believe that being a badass means that you are actually supersensitive to your own feelings, as well as ultraempathetic to the feelings of others. But if you're in a relationship where you find yourself slowly loosening your boundaries to accommodate your partner, you need to stop, look, and listen . . . to your own badass heart and brain. If your partner has you questioning your own strength, and has you bending a little too much in his direction because he says he feels like he is losing his own identity, then I say, "Move on, sister."

YOU CAN'T CHANGE THE PERSON, SO SOMETIMES YOU JUST HAVE TO CHANGE THE PERSON YOU'RE TALKING TO.

Embracing your inner badass is a challenge, to be sure. Not everyone can accept our confidence, or our unconditional love of all things productive and positive. When we go in search of a soul mate, we need to take a quick pass on anyone who is not committed to the same life goals as we are, and we especially need to be very aware of whether a potential partner will stand beside us—and fully support us—in our pursuit of being the best badass we can be.

Many of you, as you become more of the badass-type woman you were always meant to be, will be tested by those who will try to

NEVER LOSE YOURSELF IN ANY MAN'S SHADOW.

hold you back, especially if you're already in a committed relationship. Your partner may be threatened by your newfound confidence and charisma. They may feel jealous or frustrated over your new sense of purpose. They may start pulling you back in their direction, trying to keep all that badass brilliance at bay.

To this I say, stay strong. You cannot be a badass if your lover makes you feel guilty for being your true, authentic self. If your partner does not fully support and encourage you to aspire to full badass status, you need to get out.

I was in those shoes not too long ago. I was with a guy who said he felt like he was losing himself in my shadow. I really loved him and really wanted the relationship to work, so I started letting my boundaries be pushed a little bit because I thought, *Okay, he needs to be an individual, and maybe I'm a little too much. Too badass.*

Then one day it all just sort of slapped me in the face, and I came to my senses. I was like, *What the hell am I doing? Why am I toning down my power? Why am I letting this guy do a number on me so that he can feel better about himself? Why am I wasting my time on another human being, trying to help him rise to a level where* I think *he can be when, in truth, at thirty-four, if you're not fucking there already, then good luck to you, pal!*

Phew. Rough, right? Not really. Just honest. Just me. Just necessary. Just badass.

What I'm trying to say here is that in my opinion, aligning yourself with weak people or people who make you feel guilty for being your strong badass self is, again, like Superman with Kryptonite. It can only bring you down. Steer clear of friends and lovers who are not on their own path to badassness.

Change, Change, Change

"Physician, heal thyself" is a motto that everyone in the medical community should strive to live by. Likewise for every gal who is a badass-in-training: Fix yourself.

That's the beauty of being a badass. Constantly striving to improve and better ourselves is something in which we pride ourselves. Once we stop trying to change those around us, we have more time and energy to work on changing ourselves for the better. This, of course, will also improve the lives of those around us.

You can see badasses-in-training everywhere. Watching the course of Angelina Jolie's career and personal life provides lots of good examples. I totally think that Angelina Jolie is now an authentic, genuine badass. We have watched her learn and grow in so many ways.

She didn't start off as a badass. When she was younger, it seemed like she was searching for something. But she came into her own and evolved and grew and learned from her mistakes. If you look at her growth process as a human being, it's really interesting because when she was younger she didn't appear to be as focused.

Here's a woman who seemed hell-bent on hiding her beauty and her brains. She may have thought she was being badass with her gloomy fashion choices and shocking behavior—such as wearing a gold chain around her neck that held a vial of her then husband Billy Bob Thornton's blood—but she wasn't even close.

> ONCE WE STOP TRYING TO CHANGE THOSE AROUND US, WE HAVE MORE TIME AND ENERGY TO WORK ON CHANGING OURSELVES FOR THE BETTER.

No. The moment she really stepped up to the plate and began to embrace and honor her inner badass was when she adopted the beautiful orphaned baby she had fallen in love with during a humanitarian visit to Southeast Asia.

That single act of independent action gave the world its first glimpse at just what kind of a major badass Angelina Jolie was born to be.

She followed her heart. She went against the grain. She followed her true passion: saving children. By finding and honoring her authentic self, she has blossomed into a world-class badass.

ABOVE: Even badasses have bad habits.

YOU KNOW IT'S TIME TO LEAVE WHEN . . .

1. Your needs are not being met.

2. It's all about them, all the time.

3. You can't stand the way they look when they eat (walk, talk, sleep, laugh, etc.).

4. You'd rather go on that next vacation alone than with them because you know you'd have a much better time by yourself.

5. You can easily substitute the word *date* for *vacation* in statement #4.

6. They sabotage your self-esteem (put you down, minimize your strengths and achievements, pick on you about your appearance, etc.).

7. They have a roving eye or, even worse, a roving heart.

8. They are not your biggest fan.

9. They are not your best friend.

10. You've lost that loving feeling.

Lesson learned: Be a badass. Wake up and smell the roses! Do not drag (or string) dead-end relationships along.

I am blown away by how articulate and caring she has become, especially when it comes to speaking out about her causes. Her courage is there for all to see. Her confidence is in full bloom. Is she perfect? Hell, no! Does she have control issues? Maybe. Does she struggle to keep herself healthy and happy? I don't know. Being a badass does not come easy. It takes a lot of work on yourself.

Like I said before, my road to badassness never ends. I'm pretty happy with where I am, but I can assure you that when I started I was like a little badass caterpillar in a really ugly cocoon.

No More Drama!

One of the best perks of becoming a badass gal is that you finally find yourself with a good dose of self-sufficiency, of feeling capable of taking care of yourself. I think that being a badass gives you a form of clarity and a bit of peace.

Once you begin growing into your own badassness you find that you no longer have as much drama or turmoil or chaos in your life. It's like now that you're a badass, you are able to recognize things so much faster. You're able to say to yourself, *Whoa! Hey! This is unhealthy.* Or, *This is not good for me.* You also find yourself becoming much more productive. When you're a badass you become proactive in your own life, instead of getting caught up in everyone else's.

You know who you are, you're confident, and you know what you want.

The best comparison I can make is that when I was in my twenties I found myself in really long, drawn-out, high-drama relationships. I'd have relationships that lasted seven years before I finally threw in the towel. (I'm talking about mostly romantic relationships here, but the same thing could apply to some of my female friendships.)

Now if a relationship isn't feeling healthy by the sixth month, I'm getting ready to get myself out because I have a better sense of when things aren't working.

I know what I want and need. I don't want to be with a narcissist, or with a guy who is stunted in the emotional-growth department. So if I find myself falling for these kinds of guys, I make sure it won't be for too long. How do I know if someone is a narcissist or emotionally stunted? These are the signs to look for:

1. **The world seems to revolve around them (in their own mind).**

2. **They run hot and cold. One day they love you, the next day they're distant and withholding.**

3. **They get more out of being in a relationship with you than you get out of being in a relationship with them.**

4. **You feel your strength and confidence being sapped when you're around them.**

5. **They are vague and indirect; you never quite know where you stand with them.**

This is why badass women have the edge when it comes to their relationships. They know themselves better than most people do. And they know people better than most people. Why? Because they have become more observant. They are no longer caught up in everyone else's drama, so they have eyes that can see for miles. They watch the way people act. They learn from the behavior of others.

Badasses do not stand in judgment of others. Rather, we use our energy to judge for ourselves. We know what we can and can't put up with. We can make better decisions about whether a potential relationship is worth it.

We can spot when a person of interest has issues. I like to call it "drama." If you find that you and your romantic partner are constantly involved in emotional upheavals (e.g., fits of anger, tears, accusations, avoidance, shouts of "It's over!," doors slamming, Facebook status changing every other week), then you are dealing with someone who has issues.

BADASSES DO NOT STAND IN JUDGMENT OF OTHERS.

Issues are anything that keeps a person from being their best self, i.e., a whole, emotionally healthy, happy, and loving individual. Examples can range from fear of commitment and abandonment to hard-core narcissism and sex addiction. Most often, these issues result in a lot of emotional drama when it comes to intimate relationships. They can also frequently be traced back to a trauma that occurred in childhood. This is why it is so important for a badass to focus on her own emotional health, growth, and well-being. It gives

EMOTIONAL HIJACKERS AND OTHER STRANGERS I HAVE KNOWN (AND LOVED)

You know in statement #2 on page 141, where I said, "It's all about them, all the time"? Well, that worst-case relationship scenario applies to friends as well as lovers. Don't you just hate when that shit happens? When the person you are with hijacks your emotions by somehow shifting the focus from you to them—even when you have the proverbial podium. Those people make me crazy! If I am sad, they are sadder. If I am sick, they are sicker. If I have just succeeded in a major (or even minor) accomplishment, they cut my happy story short by suddenly remembering their own similar moment of glory.

If you have a friend or a lover who constantly cuts you off by saying, "I remember the time when I . . . ," you are involved with an Emotional Hijacker, and you must cut the cord.

us an edge. It allows us to set boundaries for what we will and will not tolerate in our relationships with others.

Now that we have learned not to try to control others, we know better than to think that we can fix them.

If a potential romantic partner has difficult relationships with their family, you can see that as a potential warning signal. In fact, I would call that a big, big indicator.

Badass women need to be with loving partners who can support their badassness in all its beautiful, amazing glory. We need to seek out contenders who have already done their own work on themselves.

Being a badass woman means being in balance. It means being a fully functioning human being. It means living your life in wholeness. It means being the best you can be, and not letting anyone else drag you down. It means no drama. It means surrounding yourself with others who seek the same goals. If someone isn't into working on themselves to be the best they can be as a human being—living in full confidence and integrity and honesty and conviction—then a badass woman needs to set that person free.

No Strings Attached

Knowing when to cut and run is such a valuable asset; I can't stress its importance enough. Badass women just do not waste their time. I don't care how great the sex is or how expensive the gifts are, if there isn't any "there" there, don't waste your time in a dead-end relationship. There is so much more in life to be experienced, explored, and learned; badass gals have no interest in dragging out a relationship when it becomes clear that it's not what they want.

Badass Gals Always Trust Their Gut, or
The Fine Art of Stalking

Like every good badass gal should, I live my life by this motto:
When in doubt, check it out. This is especially true when I suspect
that my boyfriend might be, shall we say, sniffing around. For me,
stalking can sometimes be essential. Stalking is a very fine art, and
nothing to tread into lightly. I do *not* condone *Fatal Attraction*–type
stuff, and if you are prone to that, put down this book and call a
shrink ASAP!

We all have moments in the beginning stages of a relationship
where the trust hasn't been established yet and we wonder just
where the hell our guy is and what he is up to. Maybe he isn't
answering his phone; maybe his explanation of something didn't
add up. Whatever it is, you find yourself sitting around wondering
what is going on and stressing yourself out. Some women just have
a hard time trusting and need proof that they can trust; others have
been given reasons to be suspicious.

Well, you don't have to just sit there and drive yourself crazy, and
you don't have to spend money hiring a private eye. You can check it
out, and chances are you have a friend who has done it and will hold
your hand through the process. I will admit
right now that I have stalked, that I have
done drive-bys and stakeouts. I have been
proven wrong in my suspicions and I have
been proven right, but I have always, always had a friend with me.
Also, when I was proven wrong, that was it—no more stalking for
me in that relationship. The dudes proved themselves trustworthy
and proved me to be just a tiny bit nutty. So I let it go and trust.

WHEN IN DOUBT, CHECK IT OUT.

Obviously, if you truly doubt your man so much that you can't let it go, then there is a bigger problem. Maybe it's within you, maybe it's him, but either way I would say it's time to really look at your relationship and admit it might not be so healthy.

Now, for those who know when to stop stalking, here's how I do it. I call any number of my friends who all have been guilty of stalking themselves. (I prefer to go with three of my friends, because we make it fun for ourselves.) There are two guys I go with, and one girl. Charlie (female) is unbelievably good at this. She is like a detective and actually could make a lot of money being a private eye. I go with her when I think my suspicion is very solid and the guy is a bit tricky. I rarely do this sort of stalking and can remember only one time we did this for me. My suspicions of cheating were right, and I was glad I had a friend with me who stopped me from getting out of the car and confronting him, further humiliating myself.

THE ESSENTIALS OF STALKING: 1) GOOD FRIENDS 2) TASTY SNACKS AND BEVERAGES 3) LOTS OF PATIENCE

Most of the time, I go with my friend Gary or my friend Roger. We have fun because we put on wigs and glasses, get bad magazines, and bring along food and drinks—you know, the basic stakeout supplies. The key is to never get caught, and if you do, to have an excuse for why you are at his house: a basket of cookies, soup if he claimed to be "sick"—anything that can somewhat justify why your crazy ass is down the street from his house. Never, *never* go in your own car or in a car he knows well. Borrow your friend's car and be polite and considerate and pay for the gas. (Yes, even in stalking there are manners.)

Make sure the friend you have chosen is supportive, fun, and—most important—a calm person with good judgment who knows when to restrain you. Also make sure they have the patience for the job, because let me tell you, it can take a while.

If he's out with friends, who knows what time he is coming home? And since you don't want to have to repeat this episode again, you want to make sure you get it right this one time. You don't want a friend who is antsy and is like, "Oh, I'm hungry and bored. Let's go to McDonald's real quick then come right back." Um, you may miss your opportunity, and then you'll have to waste more of your time on this nonsense.

Find a good spot with a clear view of his house, car, bar—wherever it is you have decided to stake out. Make sure your spot is somewhat hidden. Put on your wigs and have fun—keep the mood light and entertaining. If he is innocent, stop this craziness and just be in the relationship. If he is guilty of cheating, have your friend drive you home, stay with you, and restrain you from confronting him right away. Maybe he lied to you about who he was with or where he was going or what time he would be home. Give him a chance to tell you the truth; I mean, after all, plans *do* change, and he might not have thought to hassle you with small changes. If he lies to you . . . well, there's your answer.

Again, I do not condone crazy-ass behavior that is harmful to anyone, much less yourself, but I also don't believe in sitting around with questions that you can easily get answers to on your own.

Sometimes a Girl's Got to Be Gonzo

Just like a good Girl Scout, a badass gal needs to be prepared when she decides it's high time to bail out of a bad relationship. It's never an easy thing to do, and sometimes a girl's just got to take matters into her own hands.

TOP 5 TIPS
FOR BREAKING UP

1. DON'T EVER LET IT GET UGLY.

2. BE HONEST.

3. BE GENTLE.

4. BE PREPARED.

5. BE SWIFT AND SURE.

BEST BADASS BREAKUP SONG OF ALL TIME

"Since U Been Gone" by Kelly Clarkson

BADASS HALL OF FAMER

"I Am Woman" by Helen Reddy

BEST BADASS SONG SUNG BY A BADASS GUY

"The Unforgettable Fire" by U2

BEST BADASS OLD-SCHOOL RULE TO LIVE BY

"Fool me once, shame on you. Fool me twice, shame on me."

BEST BADASS GAL THEME SONG

"Lotta Love to Give" by Daniel Lanois

One of the best badasses I know made a clean break from her own half-baked Dough Boy of a husband (who, after two years of marriage counseling, was still refusing to admit that their marriage was dead as a doornail) by making her "great escape" this way: After getting her own finances in order (saving up enough cash to rent a small spare bedroom in the loft of an old friend for at least six months), she waited for her Wall Street hubby to leave for work on "Getaway Monday" and kicked into high gear. Having done her homework the previous week, she:

1. **Alerted the two guys with a truck that the coast was clear; they were parked a couple of blocks away in anticipation of her call.**

2. **Corralled her two cats into their carrying cases.**

3. **Put big Post-it notes on everything she wanted the movers to take. (She left most of the furniture because it had been her husband's when they married, but took the brand-new sofa bed she had wisely insisted they purchase, knowing full well that she would soon be moving out.)**

4. **Left a "nice" note on the kitchen counter, saying: "Sorry. We [she and the cats] just couldn't stay another day. Be careful. I'll be in touch."**

She made her break the badass way. She got herself out of there. She (and her cats and the new sofa bed) were safe and sound in their new place and their new life before the guy even knew what hit him. A badass gal takes care of business—by any means necessary.

Professional Relationships

Unfortunately, relationships in the workplace can pose a bit of a challenge for the badass woman. Poise, composure, and perseverance must be applied. More often than not, we need to be a great team player, even when we are the leader. Our freedom to speak our truth and to stick to our convictions can often be curtailed (if we want to keep that paycheck coming in).

But we always make sure that our own unique style and personal philosophies are fully integrated into every professional thing we do. In fact, we become known by our badass personality. Our integrity. Our authenticity. Our preparedness. Our courage. Our personality.

A badass woman in business is an employee who always delivers. She shows up on time. She accepts and follows through on her responsibilities. She never gossips or plays games. She knows her shit. She knows her competition, her audience, her marketplace, and her goals. She always strives to make her boss look good. And if she's the boss, she always treats her staff with respect. She never over-promises. She manages to integrate her personal style into everything she presents. She treats her colleagues with respect. She commands respect. Her reputation in her given field is one of genuine excellence.

Badasses get the job done. They do it with polish. They do it with pizzazz. Badass employees are memorable employees. Their self-esteem and overall expertise always shine through in everything they do. They try their best to get along with everyone. But sometimes that is not possible.

A BADASS MANAGES TO INTEGRATE HER PERSONAL STYLE INTO EVERYTHING SHE PRESENTS.

Working It at Work

Work should be rewarding even if you are working your ass off every day. Regardless of what you do professionally, even if it's not your dream job, work should still fill you with some form of pride. The fact that you are supporting yourself or contributing to a household should make you feel proud. If that's not the case, there is something wrong, and maybe the wrong is within you. Maybe you don't like to work; maybe you don't have any pride or take pride in yourself; maybe you don't want to learn how to be proud. If any of those things is true for you, take

> **WORK SHOULD BE REWARDING EVEN IF YOU ARE WORKING YOUR ASS OFF EVERY DAY.**

ABOVE: Working in New Zealand on the movie set of *Kiss Me Deadly* with (from left to right) my two costars, Robert Gant and John Rhys-Davies, along with director, Ron Oliver.

this book and dump it in the trash because you, my dear, will never be a badass.

I know some pretty badass women whose job it is to take care of the house, pay the bills on time, and raise the kids right, and those women take pride in everything they do. My mother's job is to take care of my dad; she makes his doctors' appointments and drives him there, makes sure his meds are right and taken on time, and makes sure that he eats well—and she does it with class and pride and love. That is BADASS! My dad is a fighter, and his job is to stay alive through countless strokes, heart attacks, bypass surgeries, and kidney failures, and to put up with my mom 24/7. He does

ABOVE: Badasses surround themselves with other badasses at work or at play; David Vigliano is a kick-ass literary agent.

A BADASS

WOMAN

KNOWS

HER VALUE.

it all with pride and humor and that, my friends, is BADASS. See, you don't have to work at some fancy job earning a ton of money or be famous; it's all about taking pride in what you do and doing it with everything you have, giving a hundred percent.

I have a friend named Roxana who no matter what she does gives it her all. She started as an actor and had great success for a bit. She then moved into the clothing business, becoming a publicist. It may not have been her dream job, but she did it unbelievably well and embraced it with the same enthusiasm she had for acting. She is now a handbag designer and doing well. That doesn't mean she doesn't struggle, as we all do when starting a new company, but as with everything she does in life, she gives it her all and does it with a tenacity I admire. (By the way, her handbags are amazing, as are her accessories.) She is creative and strong and never gives up. She never looks to anyone else to help her or support her, instead relying on herself to make it.

YOU DON'T HAVE TO WORK AT SOME FANCY JOB EARNING A TON OF MONEY OR BE FAMOUS; IT'S ALL ABOUT TAKING PRIDE IN WHAT YOU DO DO AND DOING IT WITH EVERYTHING YOU HAVE, GIVING A HUNDRED PERCENT.

There is, of course, the opposite of that, the woman who has a job until she meets a man, gets married, tries a new business with little true effort, fails, and instead of picking herself up and starting over, decides to do nothing, letting herself become dependent and without dreams and goals of her own. Then she expects her man to pay for her lifestyle.

As I have said before, if you are a stay-at-home mom who raises children, takes time with them, teaches and loves them, I believe

ON BEING OBSERVANT: A TRUE STORY

I met a badass gal recently when my Internet service went out. There I was, stuck at home, trying to write this book, when my computer went on the fritz. I called the company that sold me the computer, and I was told I needed to make an appointment. Being a busy badass, I didn't have time to wait, so I called my boyfriend, my dad, my friends, everyone I knew to see if someone could help me. No luck. No one knew how to solve the problem.

Finally, being the observant badass gal that I am, I remembered that I'd seen a cable service truck down the block, and that reminded me that the repair person for said local cable service had left her card in my mailbox to notify me that they would be working in our neighborhood for the next two weeks.

Within twenty minutes of my dialing the repair person's number she was knocking on my door, toolbox in hand. Five minutes later, she had solved the problem with my computer. After a round of high-fives, I told her how impressed I was and how cool it was that she was a woman, since I had never seen a female cable repair person before.

She replied by saying that she learned it all by watching her ex-boyfriend do the job when he was an independent contractor for the local cable company. Explaining that she often went along with him on his runs, she confirmed that she was the first and only female cable repair person in the county. She loved her job. She beamed with pride. She was badass all the way.

that is the hardest job there is, as well as being a very respectable one. It's the women who do nothing and expect a man to pay for everything who irk me, the way it makes all women look, the way the divorce courts handle that situation, allowing a woman (or a man, for that matter) to sit on their ass and receive a paycheck. It's so uncivilized. We as women have fought hard for equal rights and to be taken seriously in a man's world; women have marched for us, have protested for the rights we have now, and yet we still have women who expect men to take care of them. I don't care if you try something and fail, as long as you gave it

> IT'S THE WOMEN WHO DO NOTHING AND EXPECT A MAN TO PAY FOR EVERYTHING WHO IRK ME.

a hundred percent and don't sit back feeling sorry for yourself. Try, try, try again! Never give up. We all fail at something at some point in our lives; it's the women who keep trying that become great and respectable, if only to themselves.

When to Lay Down the Law

As the job market continues to tighten with more and more layoffs fueling the unemployment lines, it's definitely hunker-down time for most badass women in the job force. That said, there are times when enough is enough and a badass just has to put her foot down—even if it means she has to walk.

I say this is definitely the case if someone in your world is trying to intentionally destroy your confidence. Sometimes this is a very subtle form of **professional sabotage** that takes place over a long period of time. You've all seen or experienced it for yourself, I'm sure. You know, it's the case of somebody (usually a superior) telling you, "You were just a little too controlling here, or a little too stringent there. You've been too this. You were too that."

Even the strongest badasses I know will eventually succumb to these attacks on their self-esteem. **Over time it seeps into your brain.** You listen to it every day, and then you sleep on it, and the next thing you know, you're like, *God, you know, maybe I really* am *all those things.*

If you find yourself in a situation like that, dust off your résumé and start looking elsewhere. Now, I wouldn't advise you to quit your job before finding a new one, especially in these hard times, but give yourself the opportunity to look for something better, something that supports who you are.

If you feel a general lack of support for who you are and what you bring to your particular position, you're working in the wrong place and with the wrong people. A badass woman knows her value. She knows her worth.

For me, now more than ever, I say to myself: *If they don't appreciate this, the entire Shannen Doherty package, then they're not right for me.* The minute someone starts telling me I'm too this or too that, I have to walk away. I can't let that negativity permeate my brain, no matter how great the gig or how much I need the money. I'm not saying that you should just bail on your job and that everyone should be expected to deal with your quirks and foibles. Of course, when you're working with other people and dealing with their personalities, you have to be a collaborative person, willing to listen to others' ideas and be objective. With that being said, if there is no room for growth because your

BE STRONG. BE THE SURVIVOR.

boss doesn't believe in you, doesn't like you, or has a thing against women, then perhaps it's a good idea to leave. It is important to be happy in your job and take pride in it. It may not be your dream job, but it pays the bills, so give it everything you have.

I realize that this might not be immediately possible for every underappreciated badass gal in the workplace. If you find yourself in that boat, where you're in the trenches with some seriously difficult people at work but you have mouths to feed and you're in charge of the rent, that's when you just have to embrace your inner badass more than at any other time. Be strong. Be the survivor. If those people try to clash with you, let them know that you hear what they are saying. Look them in the eye and listen to them so that they feel they are being acknowledged. Just make sure you do not engage. Don't go toe-to-toe. Do not take the bait!

Just buckle down and do your job as best as you can. Don't let someone you dislike make you leave a job you really need. Don't let them win.

Make a Bad Situation Work for You

Since being a great badass means taking advantage of everything you can learn about a certain subject, situation, person, or pattern of behavior, when you find yourself in a bad place with your career, try to find a way to get something positive out of it.

I think the best work I have done in acting was when I was going through some sort of turmoil on the set and I was like, *Okay, how do I make this good?* I would take my difficulty in collaborating with someone and incorporate that energy or emotion into my acting. I'd work it into everything I did on set that day. This technique produced some pretty amazing moments in my career. Being badass means you take the negative and turn it into something positive. It means not being confrontational just because you are in a foul mood, but rather recognizing your foul mood and being even more open to counteracting it.

For me, if I was in turmoil because my dad was in the hospital but I still had to be at work on a set, I would let it come out in my acting. I remember on *Charmed* I had a scene where I was upset over Andy (my former boyfriend on the show) dying, and feeling like it was my fault. It was a hard day for me because my dad was very ill, in the hospital, and my best friend, who was on the show with me, wasn't speaking to me over a misunderstanding. I felt alienated and alone and, most important, just hurt and scared. I decided that my emotions should only come out in the scene, and to this day I think it was one of my most honest moments as an actor, and one of my best. Everything I was feeling was in that scene in the most pure way, and when I was done with it I was able to breathe and relax enough to keep going with the day's work. It was an outlet, and a healthy one.

If you have a difficult boss or colleagues, practice your fine art of badass management skills with them. Make them feel heard and understood, but don't engage them in battle. **Integrity will always win out in the end,** so always stay true to yourself. If you and your work are not being appreciated, start looking elsewhere, but never quit your job until you are financially prepared to go.

Remember that your self-esteem is worth money in the bank, so never let anyone get away with stealing it.

STICK TO YOUR GUNS.

REMEMBER THAT YOUR SELF-ESTEEM IS WORTH MONEY IN THE BANK, SO NEVER LET ANYONE GET AWAY WITH STEALING IT.

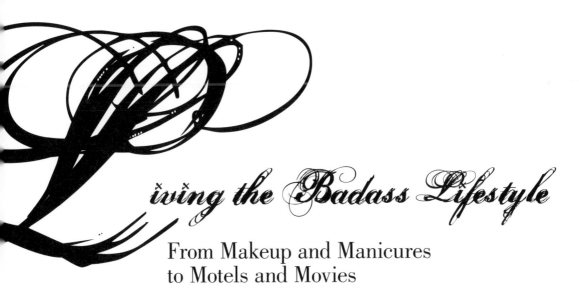

Living the Badass Lifestyle

From Makeup and Manicures to Motels and Movies

Now that you are well on your way to becoming your badass self, go ahead and start thinking more out of the box when it comes to creating your new lifestyle. Leave your worries behind when it comes to breaking the rules about things like decorating your home or throwing a badass party. Unlike the Martha Stewarts of the world, who are looking for cookie-cutter style and perfection, badass gals do things in their own individual way. (With that being said, I do consider Martha to be a badass, and that perfection is her own individual way; she has turned it into a very successful career.)

The lifestyle of a badass is as unique as the individual, but it always reflects the individual's distinct personality. You won't find a true badass ordering an entire living room set from an IKEA catalog and placing it as is in her home. In fact, she'd rather be caught dead. An authentic badass is a breed of her own—she mixes and matches, keeping a keen eye trained on what makes her happy.

The same can be said for a badass on vacation. Yes, we all like five-star resorts, but adventure is always the key. A badass will usually find herself in some remote, not often traveled to place, off the beaten path somewhere, exploring and delving into the real soul of the place she finds herself in.

Dinner parties will be unique and reflective of her own taste. Food is an experience and sometimes risky, but always fun. My point is, a badass thinks outside the box; therefore, everything she does is unconventional. It's her own individual blend of yin and yang at its best.

It's her look. Her Style. Her calling card.

Badasses embrace their own personal taste with a vengeance, and they wear it well. Why? How? Because they own it, from their hairstyle to the way they mix tattered and ratty jeans with their favorite fine white French linen blouse, sky-high red patent-leather stiletto heels, and their ex-boyfriend's broken-in black leather jacket.

As with everything badass, living the lifestyle is all about knowing what you love and who you really are. It's about loving yourself, trusting yourself, and strutting your stuff. It's about being the best you can be. It's about being resourceful and resilient. It's about having fun and inspiring others. It's about having no regrets and making no apologies—laughing at yourself and accepting your eccentricities. It's about shouting your creativity from the rooftop—if that's your style— or quietly applying that certain special something to absolutely everything you do.

The badass gal lifestyle is about doing things with panache and class, without ever having to resort to maxing out (or even using) your credit cards. In fact, never will a true badass woman pay more than she needs to for what she wants. Being frugal and always finding a bargain is just a totally badass thing to do.

Now that you have learned the basics of becoming the genuine badass woman you were always born to be—by breaking out of the shell of your former self (be it bad girl, bitch, shrinking violet, or people-pleaser) and learning my tips about how to best use your newborn badass skills when it comes to relationships—you're ready to show the world the real you, whether you are just grabbing a bite to eat with friends or doing your nails.

You're ready to Start living the badaSS lifeStyle.

This applies to everything that makes you, you.

- **From the clothes you wear**

- **To the way you entertain**

- **To the style in which you decorate**

- **To the cars you drive (and how you buy them)**

- **To the signature cakes and bread you bake (or buy)**

- **To the instant covered patios you learn how to make**

- **To the new uses for bamboo that make your friends say, "Wow! Who knew?"**

- **To the pets you own and love**

- **To the vacations you take**

- **To the lipstick you choose**

- **To the wine you drink, and**

- **To the way you work out the kinks.**

Discovering Your Own Sense of Personal Style

Focus on identifying what cultural "type" best defines the real you and use it as the basis of the badass sense of style you want to cultivate, from the way you look to the way you entertain. But don't feel the need to choose only one style everyday for everything. In my case, I definitely drift to the Bohemian sensibilities in my decorating and parties and am more classic in my dress. Badasses come in all shades, sizes, and styles. You may feel more in tune with other looks, like retro, whimsical, *Mad Men* sophisticated, modern, clean-cut preppy, art-school sloppy, chic, ghetto fabulous, goth punk, rock star, hippie chick, Earth mother, and so on. Retro girls feel at home in vintage stores, but ghetto fabulous gals, not so much.

You don't need me to tell you what the characteristics of each type are. If you're that type, you will know immediately when you see it. Just flip open any fashion magazine. The style and design will speak to you. The beauty of categorizing your type is that it makes life simple. It keeps everything about who you are and how you express yourself authentic. Sure, we all vary from our traditional ways now and then, but in general we are who we are, through and through.

So when I need to find a new gown for a big awards ceremony, you'll see me searching the more classic styles first. I know from experience that's where I pretty much always find what I like and what looks best on me.

Badass Beauty Secrets

Every genuine badass gal I know has developed her own list of
what works for her and what doesn't when it comes to being the best
she can be in the beauty department. Once again, it all boils down
to what works for you and what doesn't, what suits your personality
and what doesn't. Remember, to thine
own self be true.

The only real common denominators
of beauty tips and secrets among badasses is that we never overpay or overdo it.
And we try to live by the old adage that
you never know whom you might run
into, so we always strive to look our
best—even if we're just running out to
buy a carton of milk.

A badass gal is also great when it
comes to being beautiful on the fly. Once again, we know how to get
the job done. We keep a supply of essentials on hand in the glove
compartment of our car: mascara, lipstick, deodorant, perfume,
tweezers, hair spray, lint brush, and a spare comb.

No matter what is going on in our lives, we always make sure
that we have great shoes, purses, hairstyles, and nails. These
items will make you look pulled together and polished, no matter
if you feel that way or not. Awesome shoes and statement purses
add instant style and demand attention in a good way, so make
sure you have go-to fabulous accessories that become a permanent

OPPOSITE: Laurent D doing my hair while the stylist Deborah Waknin prepped me at a
photo shoot for *InStyle* magazine. In between shots my mom snapped this picture.

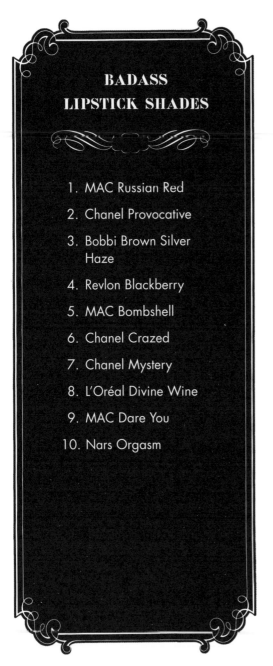

part of your look. Every badass girl should pay attention to her hair and nails. Too many women out there let these things go, many times saying that the "natural look" is a beautiful look itself. Okay, maybe if you're a granola girl, but a badass gal always maintains an extra level of style and finesse. Again, you never know whom you may run into!

If your budget doesn't allow you to splurge on designer brands, check them out at the makeup counter and then find a less expensive brand to substitute accordingly.

No-Fuss Do-It-Yourself French Manicure

One of my best friends told me about the time she was lucky enough to meet the drop-dead gorgeous and totally glamorous wife of one of the most famous best-selling novelists in the world. My friend happened to be sitting in a café in New York City at a small table next to where the wife of the famous writer was sitting (the writer was across the room being interviewed about his newest blockbuster book by a film crew from the nightly news).

After exchanging hellos, my friend told the glamorous wife that she was a big fan of her husband's books, and the next thing she knew they were gabbing together like long-lost friends. Suddenly the glamorous wife said, "Hey, wanna know how I keep my nails looking so good?" Sure, my friend said. Why not?

With that, the glamorous wife grabbed my friend's left hand, reached into her purse, pulled out a bottle of clear nail polish, and began painting it on my pal's nails. "Blow on them till they are dry," said the obviously serious badass wife of the world-famous writer.

BADASS NAIL SHADES

1. Chanel Vamp
2. MAC Dry Martini
3. Sally Hansen Gunmetal
4. Orly Witch's Blue
5. Dior Vernis Black Sequins
6. MAC Dark Angel
7. Essie Lollipop
8. OPI Suzi Says Da
9. Chanel Vendetta
10. Chanel Forbidden

Next thing she knew, Mrs. Badass pulled a white Sharpie felt pen from her big black crocodile purse and began drawing little white half moons across the top of each nail. A second application of quick-drying top coat, and voilà!—instant badass fabulosity! A French manicure done not only on the fly, but on a budget.

Better Homes and Badasses

My home is a reflection of me and is best described as eclectic, with a mishmash of things I have collected over many years all blending together, but always catching the eye. I have very expensive antique pieces sitting right next to the credenza I got at a big-box store a few years ago. I have flea-market pieces next to signed Salvador Dalí paintings. **High-low is my style.** I work hard and am proud I can afford the nicer things that catch my eye. But just because I can afford something expensive doesn't mean I'm stupid about money. Badasses like to get the most out of life, and they also like to get the most out of their dollars. It's not about how much you spend, but about having your personality stamped all over your home.

The one thing that all badass women know and love is owning and sharing that feeling of being down-to-earth at all times, of creating or visiting a place or space where those you love and enjoy can also feel warm and happy and well cared for and divine in their own skin and surroundings.

Whether you are decorating your dorm room or want to update your living space to reflect your new badass persona, identifying your top five favorite items that you own will help you put the

ABOVE: My home is my refuge, so I make it as comfortable as possible.

finishing touches on your decorating scheme. I don't live by any hard-and-fast rules when it comes to decorating, so I wouldn't suggest that you group those five things together and buy everything along those same styles. Boring! Instead, make your favorite things a focal point in your home. If you happen to fall in love with an antique weathervane, hang it above the couch as if it were artwork. Finding a way to use or display something other than as intended is totally badass.

ABOVE: Filling your home with photos of happy times will help you keep a smile on your face and thinking positively.

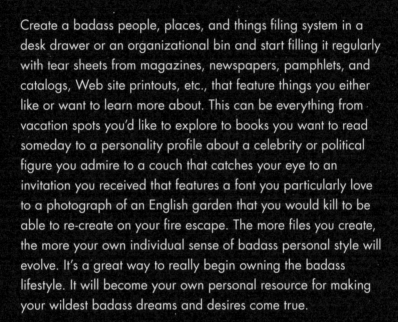

FUN FILES

Create a badass people, places, and things filing system in a desk drawer or an organizational bin and start filling it regularly with tear sheets from magazines, newspapers, pamphlets, and catalogs, Web site printouts, etc., that feature things you either like or want to learn more about. This can be everything from vacation spots you'd like to explore to books you want to read someday to a personality profile about a celebrity or political figure you admire to a couch that catches your eye to an invitation you received that features a font you particularly love to a photograph of an English garden that you would kill to be able to re-create on your fire escape. The more files you create, the more your own individual sense of badass personal style will evolve. It's a great way to really begin owning the badass lifestyle. It will become your own personal resource for making your wildest badass dreams and desires come true.

WHAT?

YOU DON'T

CREATIVE

YOUR BODY?

THINK

YOU SAY HAVE A BONE IN WELL, AGAIN!

Badass Décor

How many times have you walked into an apartment, house, restaurant, hotel, etc., and just been hit with the wow factor? A badass knows that in order to create an amazing space for herself as well as for others, she must embrace her own unique creative force.

What? You say you don't have a creative bone in your body? Well, think again! **Some of the most disregarded items can be transformed to create an environment that you thrive in.** Did you ever play house as a child, or build a fort or clubhouse? Think about what you did to create that space. A sheet became a curtain, a telephone cable spool became a table, a large bowl served as a sink, tree stumps were used as stools, jars were vases filled with wildflowers. Well, you might be all grown up, but the concept is still the same.

Whenever you step into a store or flea market, let your imagination run wild, just like when you were a kid. Could that antique flowerpot stand make a cool glass-topped side table? Maybe a discarded pie safe from the '50s would be a neat place to store linens. Or that ultramodern sofa could look really awesome next to your vintage Danish Modern chairs. Be creative and let your true badass self show in your design sense. It's all about inspiration, aspiration, and improvisation!

Pretty Patios in a Pinch

Every badass likes to throw a good party (see page 195 for tips), and that means that you also want the space and the décor to be a

ABOVE: In decorating, it's fun to group different things together to tell a story.

OVERLEAF: The colors of this antique chandelier from the 1920s complement a photo taken by Kurt Iswarienko.

little different—and definitely awesome. I love creating a comfy environment for friends and family, especially when I haven't overextended myself. Remember, a badass knows her limits. Creating a room outdoors will extend your entertaining area, so if you do not have a covered patio space, make one.

This can be done relatively inexpensively by first constructing a point of focus. To do so you will need four large coffee cans (or something similar), four bamboo poles, a bag of self-setting cement or sand, and some fabric (a sheet or sheer curtains would work well, but whatever fabric you choose, make sure it is bright and airy, and not too heavy). First you'll want to paint or decorate the cans to match your décor. If you are handy with a glue gun, this is the perfect use for all the broken plates, wine corks, foreign coins, etc., you've been collecting but didn't know what to do with. Drill a quarter-inch hole through the top of each of the bambo poles.

CREATING A ROOM OUTDOORS WILL EXTEND YOUR ENTERTAINING AREA, SO IF YOU DO NOT HAVE A COVERED PATIO SPACE, MAKE ONE.

Next, take the fabric and put some ties on each corner. If you're using a vintage sheet, tie about twelve inches of twine, yarn, or ribbon to each corner. If you're really crafty, a nice touch is to make matching ties. The ties are what will be anchoring the fabric to the poles, so you'll want to make sure they're securely fastened to the sheet. (The heavier the fabric, the more concerned you should be about making sure the ties aren't going to pull away from it.)

Then put the concrete (or sand) into the cans and set your bamboo poles in them. Space the cans evenly apart in a square (or whatever size or shape your fabric is). If you are a black belt in badass and are using concrete, you have to wait until the concrete has hardened in the cans. Finally, run your fabric ties through each of the holes. Now you have your focal point. You can arrange a table and chairs under it, or throw a bunch of colorful pillows around, Moroccan style.

ABOVE: A badass view speaks for itself when entertaining outdoors. Don't overdo your décor if you have a killer natural landscape.

Making Badass Magic with Vintage Fabric

I love shopping at swap meets and flea markets because of the high probability that I will find something unique. Keeping a badass edge means we don't want to have what everyone else does. In addition to offering cool odds and ends, places like swap meets and flea markets are great places to find vintage fabrics, or even vintage draperies. And having a stash of unique fabrics can really help you give your home a little makeover, without spending tons of cash.

If you happen to find a fabric or drapery that you like, but there is not enough for all your windows, get it anyway. You can combine it with shutters, blinds, or sheers, using the vintage fabric or drapery as the accent for the window by draping a little of it over the top of the window. Curtain rods can be expensive, but who says you have to buy them as is in the store? What are they really but just a bunch of poles and some hardware? (Badasses see things for what they are!) You can create your own rods by using bamboo poles, or any kind of piping, attached to the wall with some hooks. What you use depends on your style and what you are trying to create.

And uses for drapes don't stop at the windows. The pleats of vintage draperies can be taken out and the drapes placed over the back of a sofa for an accent, or the fabric can be draped, tucked, and pinned, and voilà—instant slipcover. Or cut up the fabric and sew some pillows to throw on your couch. Or just throw it on a table and it becomes a tablecloth. A little bit of awesome fabric can go a long way in adding personality to your home. Before you know it, you have created a super badass and romantic area in your garden or on your patio.

Sit on It

Mismatched chairs are masterpieces waiting to happen. Don't be afraid to pick up that discarded chair on the street. A hammer, nails, some carpenter glue, and paint will come together to give you a very usable item, either in your home or in your garden. A certain company that we are all familiar with made a fortune painting items white and using just a few colored accessories. This is the easiest thing for you to do—paint it white. However, to give each chair its own story is not only fun for your creative mind but also creates conversation among your guests.

I had a ranch house a while back where barbecue parties happened regularly. I found a very long table at a flea market and refinished it with a dark walnut stain. I then collected an assortment of unfinished chairs from a going-out-of-business sale. I was out of town for a month working, and when I came back, my mom, Rosa, had painted the chairs different colors—olive green, azure blue, muted red. We then went to a discount store and found various colorful, patterned throw pillows to go in them.

You could do this same thing with a picnic table if you wanted. Stain or paint it, then make cushions for the benches with foam rubber and fabric. Add a unique chair to each end of the table. Or add chairs all around. The chairs at the end can be stenciled or hand-painted with unique designs. All that matters is that you put your own badass stamp on your home, inside and out.

Now, That's Entertainment!

With your head on straight, good people in your life, and your pad looking good, it's time to open up your home to friends and family.

ABOVE: Every badass needs good friends, and my dear friend Roger is as good as they get.

ABOVE: Roxana Zal has been my friend for more than twenty years. Here we are out to dinner in New York.

Entertaining at home is one of my favorite ways to see people. It's comfortable, relaxing, and, most of all, real, because I don't get caught up with the details of everything being perfect. Your guests will have fun if you are having fun.

My dinner parties always have a slightly Bohemian feel to them, as I mix up glasses and dishes. I will have red goblets and bright blue tumblers, yellow napkins, and plates with butterflies of all different colors stamped on them. The food is rich and plentiful, and the evening usually ends in a game of charades or Rock Band.

It is me in a nutshell, and I always make sure that people feel comfortable and warm in my surroundings. You'll find large and small pillows and blankets in virtually every room in my home. I always have a good stash of wine, beer, bottled water, soda, ice, nuts, and cheese and crackers tucked away in case of unexpected visitors. Ditto for my pantry, which is always stocked with something good I can pull together fast for famished friends and relatives. I even picked up some extra luxurious robes, nightgowns, and pajamas when they went on sale at my favorite high-end shop, for those nights when people hadn't planned on not driving home.

Badass Party Planning, Shannen-Style

Throwing a party can be as easy or as hard as you choose to make it. Just be sure that it reflects you and that you're comfortable with the decisions you make. If you're the Bohemian type, then a certain funkiness will add to the flair. If you're more a retro kind of gal, break out all your best midcentury accessories—and make sure to wear a beehive hairdo and your sexiest waist-cinching hostess apron to impress your guests. Is your personal style chic and sophisticated? Then you absolutely must mix martinis and serve fancy little canapés with olives, and offer a nice cheese tray.

Small, intimate dinner parties are my favorite, and what I lean toward. I have also thrown larger parties with great success and little stress on myself emotionally—and on my wallet. Here are some tips for both.

Small Dinner Party

For a little soiree, I keep the guest list to ten people, tops, and I try to invite some good conversationalists to keep the talk going. I like the intimacy of a sit-down dinner. Having home-cooked food is a really nice touch and makes the whole evening so much more special. (I've included some of my favorite recipes starting on page 211, in case you don't have your own signature recipes yet.) Asking each couple to bring a dish that goes with the theme of the main course will also ensure that there's plenty of food, and it will take a little pressure off of you.

Other than good company, having good wine is a must. You can get good wines at very reasonable prices. Costco has a great selection of wines for not a lot of money. I've gotten a wine there from Argentina that costs less than thirty dollars and tastes like it costs three hundred. It's fantastic. There is also some great value in Spanish wine, including Rioja and Ribera del Duero that costs around ten dollars. As with all things badass, it's not how much you spend that counts, so decant the wines. There is no need for anyone to know how much or where you got them from. Besides, it'll help the wines breathe and make them taste better.

ABOVE: Entertaining at home is my favorite way to spend time with friends.

IT'S NOT
HOW MUCH
YOU SPEND
THAT COUNTS,
IT'S HOW
YOU
SPEND IT
THAT
MATTERS.

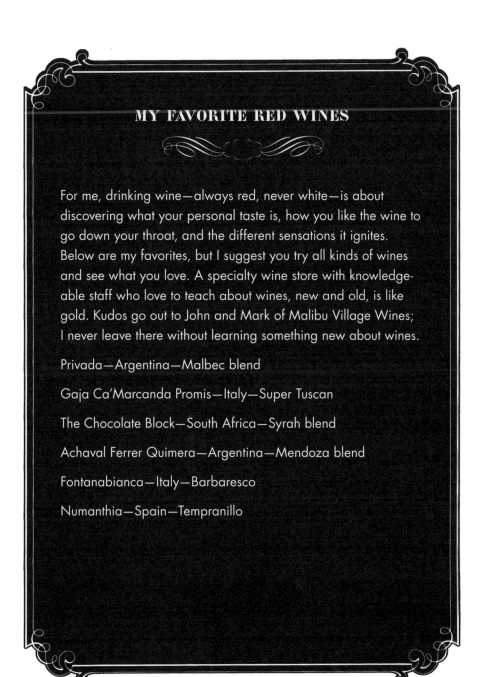

MY FAVORITE RED WINES

For me, drinking wine—always red, never white—is about discovering what your personal taste is, how you like the wine to go down your throat, and the different sensations it ignites. Below are my favorites, but I suggest you try all kinds of wines and see what you love. A specialty wine store with knowledge-able staff who love to teach about wines, new and old, is like gold. Kudos go out to John and Mark of Malibu Village Wines; I never leave there without learning something new about wines.

Privada—Argentina—Malbec blend

Gaja Ca'Marcanda Promis—Italy—Super Tuscan

The Chocolate Block—South Africa—Syrah blend

Achaval Ferrer Quimera—Argentina—Mendoza blend

Fontanabianca—Italy—Barbaresco

Numanthia—Spain—Tempranillo

It's amazing how you can set the mood with a little music and the right lighting. Always have good music playing in the background, but not so loud that your guests have to shout to talk to one another. If you have overhead lights, you should dim them, or use accent lighting. Light candles—everyone looks good in candlelight, and it creates a really cozy mood. But just remember that scented candles aren't a good idea where people are eating because the smell will throw off the taste of your scrumptious food. Scented candles are a great touch in the bathroom and bedroom, though.

Have an after-dinner game to play, like charades or Rock Band. Charades is one of my favorites, because you don't need to have anything ready ahead of time. Most everyone knows the rules, and if they don't, they're pretty simple to learn—keep your mouth shut while trying to act out something.

Oh, and never forget to offer doggie bags at the end of the night. Who doesn't love a little late-night or early-morning nibble after great badasses like us throw a party? That's why I like to have lots of spare Chinese take-out containers on hand, and I always have plenty of plastic wrap, aluminum foil, and a big box of quart-sized freezer bags. (The freezer bags are particularly useful when I have to get on a commercial flight and carry on all those little bits of makeup, lotions, and potions through security.)

Large Parties

I recently had a big bash for a friend of mine where I hosted around eighty people in my home. Obviously, a party of this size can get expensive, but all in all I spent a total of two thousand dollars, which for eighty people to eat, drink, and dance (DJ included) is, in

ABOVE: Being a badass host means you have a seat for every guest; not necessarily every chair needs to match.

my opinion, not too bad. You'd be hard-pressed to entertain that many people for a whole evening for less than twenty-five dollars a person. Dinner and a movie costs much more than that, and is only half as much fun!

If you're going to throw a party that big, you should consider renting tables, chairs, napkins, and silverware from a party place. That is, of course, unless you actually have service for that many people. Remember, all the plates and glasses don't necessarily have to match, but you don't want to be washing dishes in the middle of your party so you have something to serve the dessert on.

To decorate, get simple tea lights to place in the middle of each table. A little candlelight goes a long way. Definitely have fresh flowers on the tables. I went to the downtown flower mart super early in the morning and got plenty of flowers for each table at a very low cost. I already had lots of vases for my flowers, but if you don't, use mismatched containers for the flowers. Pitchers, tin cans, mason jars, etc., can add an infinite amount of charm to the tables.

Serve great comfort food, buffet-style. For the shindig I threw my friend, I had barbecue with all the fixings: corn, rolls, coleslaw, and beans. By serving filling food, chances are you won't run out because fewer people will be inclined to go back for seconds. And here's another tip: when serving corn, cut each ear in half, which means ordering less and having more servings.

Get your juices, beer, wine, and liquor at a national chain store or your favorite big-box store for a better selection and discount. You can hire a bartender for fairly little money. You don't have to hire a professional; I am sure someone you know knows someone who would love to make some easy money for the night as a freelance bartender or server. I chose not to have a bartender. Instead, I bought tons of pitchers and made batches of margaritas, cosmos, mai tais, and scorpions and put them all in my outdoor refrigerator and had people help themselves. My guests loved it.

In terms of entertainment, I suggest you hire a DJ. Do your best to find a DJ who also has a karaoke machine. It's always fun to have the option of your friends letting loose and singing in front of people. Your friends are, after all, the best source of entertainment.

And finally, relax and enjoy yourself! If you are running around stressing, that is totally not badass! Your guests will pick up on your vibe, so don't be a bummer. Be a badass!

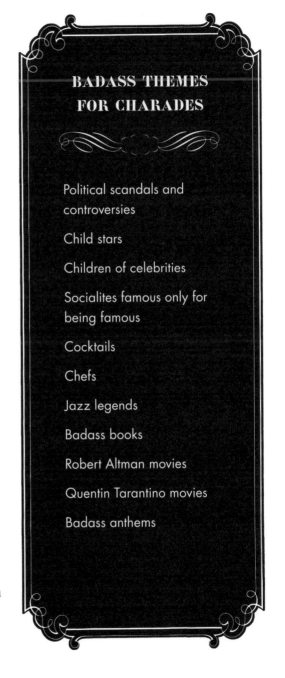

BADASS THEMES FOR CHARADES

Political scandals and controversies

Child stars

Children of celebrities

Socialites famous only for being famous

Cocktails

Chefs

Jazz legends

Badass books

Robert Altman movies

Quentin Tarantino movies

Badass anthems

ABOVE: Candlelight adds instant charm to any setting.

FLOWERS ON A DIME

Fresh flowers can add a lot of style to a place, but they also have a tendency to add to the bill. If there isn't a wholesale flower district where you live, get your blooms at the supermarket. Just stay away from common roses and carnations—they're boring. Be badass by getting a ton of baby's breath instead, and making an ethereal baby's breath–only arrangement. Ditto for ferns. If you want to get totally crafty, buy a bunch of mixed bouquets, then take them apart and make arrangements of a single flower type. A bunch of chrysanthemums or a variety of flowers all in the same color make more of an impact than a mishmash of colors.

Remember, everything doesn't have to be perfect when you're having a party. The tablecloths don't have to match, and the glasses can be all sizes, the candles all different shapes. I actually think variety adds to the charm. A badass hostess works with what she has at hand. As they say, heaven is in the details, so use your special badass touch to make your parties memorable.

BADASS PARTY SHORTCUTS

Pasta is another great idea for your next badass dinner party. It's easy to make and inexpensive, and if you don't cook, you can order fresh, delicious ravioli, stuffed shells, lasagna, etc., ahead of time from a local Italian joint. Once you pick up the food, make sure to put it in your own bowls and dishes. Ditto for Indian food, deli, Southern fried chicken, sushi, Thai, Chinese, you name it.

You can accept all the compliments if your guests dish 'em to you, but if someone asks for the recipe, you gotta get all badass on your guests and tell them the truth . . . including giving everyone take-out menus from the place you purchased from so they can go home with a tried-and-true recommendation.

If you find that your wallet is extended too much to order food from a favorite local restaurant, hightail it to Costco, my favorite big-box store, and buy prepared dishes from them. You'll find everything you need, from meatballs to pot stickers to tamales to curried chicken, all in the freezer section. Costco is great because they have really good food premade, perfect for a large number of people. Their wine is good, their sodas are cheap, and you can pretty much find everything you need to throw a party there without breaking your badass budget!

A PIZZA AND
A SIX-PACK OF
BEER CAN BE
A PARTY AS LONG
AS YOU ARE
SURROUNDED BY
YOUR FAVORITE
PEOPLE.

10 Dos and Don'ts for

1. Always have everything ready (including your own appearance) before your guests arrive, so you can immediately be part of the mixing and mingling.

2. Never say no if one of your dinner guests wants to bring a friend. If you don't have enough place settings to accommodate the extra person, just mix and match what you have on hand.

3. Always have more food and drink than you think you need.

4. Make sure you get the chance to speak to each and every person in the room.

5. Rave about each of your guests to others and introduce people to one another.

Being a Good Host

6. Insist that people take home doggie bags of leftover food. Any Chinese restaurant in the world will be happy to sell you a few dozen white cardboard take-out containers.

7. Never start cleaning up while guests are still present—unless, of course, you want them to leave.

8. Don't stress out if something isn't done the way you had hoped. Remember, if you are having fun, your guests are having fun.

9. Make sure to always have a hand towel out in the bathroom—keeping your bath towel just for you!

10. If something gets broken, clean it up quickly and don't make a big deal out of it. It's not a party unless something gets broken!

MY FAVORITE RECIPES

Contrary to popular belief, cooking is a totally badass thing to do. It can be really satisfying because you're creating something right there and then that you can very quickly enjoy and share with friends. Badasses love to improvise when cooking. If you're following a recipe, add your own flair to it. I never pay attention to measurements; instead, I do it all by taste and smell. I add things like chicken stock when water is called for, or add a little butter if the recipe calls for olive oil.

For the recipes following, I give you specific guidelines so all you baby badasses out there will be sure to get good results, but I urge you to put your own stamp on these dishes.

Perfect Roast Chicken

MAKES 2 TO 3 SERVINGS

I know there are lots of ways to roast a chicken, but I think this is the best way. Starting the recipe one day in advance gives the bird that extra je ne sais quoi.

1 2½- to 3-pound organic chicken

Gray sea salt

6 sprigs fresh thyme

The day before you plan to cook the chicken, wash and dry it completely, inside and out. Season it heavily with salt, both inside and out and under the skin. Put the chicken in a large plastic bag or place it on a baking sheet and wrap it in plastic wrap. Refrigerate it for 12 hours.

To cook the chicken, take it out of the refrigerator and let it rest at room temperature for about 45 minutes.

Preheat the oven to 500°F, or the hottest setting possible.

Set a large sauté pan over medium-high heat. When the pan is hot, put the chicken in it; cook for 5 minutes. Turn off the heat and put the pan in the oven. Roast the chicken for 10 minutes, then reduce the heat to 425°F and cook for 45 minutes to 1 hour, basting occasionally with the pan juices, until the chicken is golden brown and a meat thermometer reads 180°F when inserted into a thigh or breast.

Remove the pan from the oven and add the thyme to the pan juices. Baste the chicken again with the pan juices before serving.

My Dad's Chilean Sea Bass

MAKES 4 SERVINGS

This is really quick to make, and ideal for an impromptu gathering.

1 medium tomato, diced

1 medium sweet onion, diced

2 garlic cloves, minced

3 tablespoons olive oil

2 teaspoons ground cumin

¼ teaspoon cayenne

Salt and freshly ground black pepper, to taste

4 6-ounce fillets Chilean sea bass

2 tablespoons unsalted butter

Preheat the oven to 450°F.

Combine the tomato, onion, garlic, and 1 tablespoon of the olive oil in a medium bowl. Set aside.

Pour the remaining 2 tablespoons of olive oil onto a large plate, and season it with the cumin, cayenne, salt, and pepper. Set aside.

Put a large oven-safe skillet on the stove over high heat. Wash the fish under running water and pat it dry with paper towels. Dip both sides of a fillet in the seasoned olive oil and place it in the hot skillet. Repeat with the remaining fillets of fish (if you can't fit all four fillets in your pan, cook them in batches). Cook for 3 to 4 minutes, or until the fish is cooked halfway through. Flip the fish over, put ½ tablespoon of butter on each fillet, and put the skillet in the oven. Roast the fish for 5 to 6 minutes, or until it is firm and opaque.

Meanwhile, put the reserved tomato and onion mixture in a skillet set over medium heat. Cook for 8 to 10 minutes, or until the onion begins to soften.

To serve, place a piece of fish on a plate and spoon some of the tomato and onion mixture over the top.

Shannen's Filet Mignon Roast

MAKES 8 TO 10 SERVINGS

With a cut of meat this good, you really can't go wrong.

3½ pound filet mignon roast

3 tablespoons olive oil

Sea salt and freshly ground black pepper, to taste

5 sprigs fresh rosemary

2 garlic cloves, peeled and thinly sliced

2 cups dry red wine

1 bay leaf

4 sprigs fresh thyme

2 garlic cloves, peeled and crushed

1 stick salted butter

Preheat the oven to 350°F.

Rub the roast with the olive oil. Sprinkle with the salt and pepper, then rub it with 2 sprigs of the rosemary. Set the roast aside to marinate for 30 minutes.

With the tip of a sharp knife, make small incisions all over the roast, and insert thin slices of garlic into each incision.

Put ¼ cup of water in the bottom of a large roasting pan (the water should cover the bottom of the pan) and add the red wine, remaining 3 sprigs of rosemary, bay leaf, thyme, and crushed garlic. Slice the butter into thin pieces and add them to the water in the pan. Put the roast in the roasting pan, cover with the lid, and roast for 40 minutes, or until a meat thermometer inserted in the thickest part of the meat registers 130°F. Remember to baste the roast with the butter and wine mixture.

Remove the pan from the oven and place the roast on a cutting board. Tent with aluminum foil and let rest for 10 minutes before cutting.

Thinly slice the roast, and place on serving plates. Pour about 2 tablespoons of the pan juices over the meat and serve immediately.

Green Beans

This dish is decadent and definitely not healthy, but so worth it.

1 pound French green beans

4 tablespoons unsalted butter, melted

½ cup brown sugar

½ cup pecans

Blanch the beans in a large pot of boiling salted water for 2 minutes. Drain the beans, and immediately plunge them in a bowl of ice water. Drain again, and set aside.

Put the butter, brown sugar, and pecans in the bowl of a food processor and pulse until the mixture is well combined.

Put the beans and brown sugar mixture into a shallow sauté pan set over low heat. Stir to thoroughly coat the beans in the sauce, about 2 minutes. Serve warm.

Note: I don't usually measure my ingredients. The amount of sugar you use is up to you, so you can make the pecans as sugary as you like.

Stuffed Tomatoes

MAKES 6 SERVINGS

When I have a dinner party, I like to keep the appetizers simple because I tend to make too much food and don't want people filling up before the main course. That said, these tomatoes are great if you want something heavier.

6 large tomatoes, preferably heirloom

2 small chilies

1 pound mild Italian sausage, casings removed

1 cup bread crumbs

¼ cup plus 1 tablespoon olive oil

½ tablespoon unsalted butter

Preheat the oven to 250°F.

Cut off the tops of the tomatoes and scoop out the flesh with a spoon, reserving the flesh.

Cut off the tops of the chilies, and add the chilies, reserved tomato flesh, sausage, bread crumbs, and ¼ cup olive oil to the bowl of a food processor. Pulse until the mixture is well combined.

Place a large sauté pan over medium heat, and add the remaining 1 tablespoon of olive oil and the butter. When the pan is hot, add the sausage mixture and cook until it is just barely done, about 8 minutes. Remove from the heat and let cool slightly.

Place the hollowed-out tomatoes in a 9 x 13-inch oven-safe glass baking dish. Fill the tomatoes with the sausage mixture. Bake the tomatoes for about 25 minutes, or until heated through. Serve.

Mashed Potatoes

MAKES 4 SERVINGS

Remember, I'm Irish!

2 pounds russet potatoes, peeled and cut into quarters

1 cup milk

½ cup sour cream

4 ounces cream cheese

6 tablespoons unsalted butter

Salt, to taste

Put the potatoes in a large pot, cover them with water, and add plenty of salt. Bring the water to a boil, then simmer for about 25 minutes, or until the potatoes are very soft. Drain well and let cool slightly.

Put the potatoes in the bowl of a stand mixer and add the milk, sour cream, cream cheese, and butter. Mix just for a few minutes, until everything is combined. Season with salt.

Note: You can vary amounts of the ingredients to suit your taste.

Grannie Wright's Sweet Potato Pie

MAKES 2 9-INCH PIES

This recipe was handed down from my great-grandmother to my grandmother to my mom and then to me. I had to get special permission from my grandmother to put it in the book!

3 pounds sweet potatoes

1½ cups sugar

1 stick unsalted butter, melted

1 cup milk

3 large eggs

½ teaspoon vanilla

Dash of salt

2 9-inch store-bought piecrusts

Preheat the oven to 325°F.

Prick the sweet potatoes with a fork. Microwave them on high for 6 minutes. Turn the sweet potatoes over, and microwave for 6 more minutes. Let the sweet potatoes cool completely. Peel the skin off the sweet potatoes and mash them with a potato masher. You should have about 1½ cups of sweet potatoes.

Put the sweet potatoes, sugar, butter, milk, eggs, vanilla, and salt in a large mixing bowl, and whisk to combine. Pour the filling into the two piecrusts. Place the pies on a baking sheet, and bake for 40 minutes, or until a wooden pick inserted in the middle comes out clean.

Note: Baked or boiled sweet potatoes also work well in this pie—as do canned sweet potatoes.

ABOVE: Anne Marie Kortright and I can have fun together anywhere, out in the town or at home with her daughter—the hallmarks of true badass gals.

Being Badass When You're Out on the Town

Just ask yourself, "What would Princess Grace do?" and you pretty much have the game plan on how to behave like a first-class badass when you're out in a bar or at a restaurant. Failing that, go back and reread the three rules to being a badass, and pay particular attention to the first and last tenets—always have integrity (think about the golden rule) and radiate confidence. The key to success is to have class. Be yourself, be badass, but be kind and cordial to the waitstaff, the valet, the coat check person, or anyone else who is there to help make your night a fun one. Charm them and they will take great care of you. Not only that, you never know when your own fortunes may turn and you find yourself on the other side of the tip-receiving line.

Children aren't the only ones who need to know how to behave in a restaurant. So-called grown-ups can be the worst offenders. Many an out-of-work actor has worked in a restaurant as a waiter, so I hear horror stories of bad behavior from people who think that eating out in a nice restaurant is an excuse to act like a jerk. If you want to learn about people, just work in a restaurant for a week.

The thing about confidence is it's really important to having a good time, too. You may be a woman who is not a great dancer. That's cool. But if you're an authentic badass gal who is a bad dancer, I know people aren't going to find you sitting on the side-lines at the next family wedding or office holiday party. Hell, no—you'll be out there on the dance floor, having the time of your life. Have no fear, no stress. You're just out there making up dance moves that no one else in the world has ever seen before.

TAQUIZAS
Taco Zone
TEL. (818) 3 0 414
DOMICILIO

TACOZONE

KENANBELL

ASADA   PASTOR   CARNITAS
SUADERO LENGUA   CABEZA POLLO
TRIPAS   BUCHE   CHORIZO CHICKEN   HOT

KENANBELL

ORDENE
Y PAGUE QU
BUEN PRO E HO

GANGI

TOSTADAS DE CEVICHE DE CAMARON Y JAIBA

OPPOSITE AND ABOVE: Badasses aren't afraid to eat from taco trucks or hang out at dive bars.

Dos and Don'ts at a Restaurant

1. **Look everyone in the eye when you're speaking to them.** Just because someone is there to serve you doesn't mean you can treat them like a second-class citizen. Treat valets, hosts/hostesses, waiters/waitresses, servers/busboys, and bathroom attendants with respect.

2. **Don't ever wave or snap to call someone over if you want something.** Establishing eye contact usually does the trick.

3. **If you're asking for something special or off the menu,** realize you're being a pain in the ass and don't ever be righteous about it.

4. **Don't talk on the phone or text at the table.** If you must take a call, excuse yourself from the table.

5. **Be aware of your surroundings.** If you're in a fancy restaurant where it's all about candles and soft lighting, don't be surprised if your bachelorette party is seated by the bathrooms or the kitchen.

6. **Tip well.** If you ever have to think about leaving the extra dollar, then leave it. You won't miss it, but the waiter will.

Unwinding the Badass Way

Badasses work hard, and we play hard. So when it is time to call it a day and give ourselves a much-needed break from kicking ass and taking names, we definitely know how to relax. For me, traveling is a big part of rest and relaxation. Traveling is also crucial to expanding your horizons and really being able to broaden your view of the world. What better way to walk in someone's shoes than to actually walk in the well-worn paths of those who were there hundreds, if not thousands, of years ago? But because badasses usually break away from the pack in everything we do, vacation destinations are no exception.

We frequently take the road less traveled. We go out in search of the rare, the exotic, the new, and the authentic. We go boldly with confidence and mix and mingle effortlessly because of our keen badass skills of observation—immediately taking note of the local traditions and behaviors, and exercising our ever-vigilant respect for every human being we encounter.

TRAVELING IS ALSO CRUCIAL TO EXPANDING YOUR HORIZONS AND REALLY BEING ABLE TO BROADEN YOUR VIEW OF THE WORLD.

Take one of my recent trips to Sayulita, Mexico, for example. Not exactly what you would expect a celebrity like me to choose, right? Street vendors are all around, as are stray dogs. It's definitely not a touristy place; it's more of a local's locale. But it's places like Sayulita that I am totally drawn to: casual, colorful, and full of

OVERLEAF: Mexico is one of my favorite places to go for vacation.

surprises. They're more "me." They're where I can do what really makes me happy—in this case, finding the real heart and soul of the people, spending my free time learning something completely new, lazily falling into this strange and amazing part of Mexico, soaking up everything I can about its quirky culture, and enjoying its amazing beaches and landscapes.

As a badass, for me it's all about getting out and meeting people—driving to the house of the woman who makes the best tamales I have ever tasted; visiting the nearby watering hole with the locals and hearing them talk about the secret spots for surfing, the best beach, the best bargains, the best food, and so on. It's connecting with the heart of the place you are in and trying new things with a sense of bravery.

In short, badasses seek out vacation spots with a sense of adventure. They're also always on the lookout for places where they can experience a fresh source of knowledge. Love to hang out on the beach and soak up the sun? Head to the coast of South Africa instead of the trendy shores of Waikiki. Or check out Argentina, where you can easily take side trips to Patagonia and hike the Perito Moreno Glacier, or travel to France's southwest wine country, where you could score some incredible Malbec. Love Mexican food? Consider making a trip to Oaxaca, and take a cooking class to learn how to make a delicious mole sauce.

Enjoy boating? Instead of booking a trip on the next Princess Cruise to Puerto Rico, rent yourself some canoes and go paddling with your friends in the gorgeously untouched lakes and wilderness of northern Canada.

Top 10 Badass U.S. Vacation Destinations

1. **Jackson Hole, Wyoming**—Big mountains are pretty badass, even if you don't ski.

2. **Badlands, South Dakota**—A visit to the most badass of all prairie lands will really help you keep your life and problems in perspective.

3. **Joshua Tree, California**—Yes, there is such a thing as a real Joshua tree, and it exists only here. Go camping or spend the night in Palm Springs for a surreal adventure.

4. **Denali National Park, Alaska**—Go before it's gone.

5. **Sanibel Island, Florida**—Not at all what you would expect from a Florida beach (no girls gone wild), but the beaches will have you relaxing to the max.

6. **Kauai, Hawaii**—Mountains, beaches, waterfalls . . . Mother Nature shows you just how badass she can be.

7. **New York, New York**—Everything they say about the Big Apple is true—it's totally intense and amazing.

8. **New Orleans, Louisiana**—Be sure to expand your horizons beyond the French Quarter and check out the Garden District and aboveground cemeteries, too.

9. The Salton Sea, California—This ocean in the desert is magical, weird, and inspiring. (See the photo below.)

10. Austin, Texas—Avoid the zoo that is South by Southwest, but enjoy all the indie music, film, and fashion any other time.

Top 10 Badass International Destinations

1. **Barcelona, Spain**—A trip through this enchanted city and nearby Costa Brava region will help you appreciate why Antonio Gaudí and Salvador Dalí were such geniuses.

2. **Santa Catalina, Panama**—Amazing beaches and surf; plus, rain forests and mountains are just a hop, skip, and a jump away.

3. **Sayulita, Mexico**—The meaning of rest and relaxation can be found here.

4. **Istanbul, Turkey**—The combination of history, architecture, and culture is intoxicating.

5. **São Paulo, Brazil**—Find out why the most beautiful people on Earth have so much fun.

ABOVE: I like adventure-filled vacation places that are off-the-beaten path, like Sayulita, Mexico.

6. **Cape Town, South Africa**—This waterfront city offers something for everyone. While in the country, take a little safari (check out Kruger National Park) to help you understand why mere mortals are not kings of the jungle.

7. **Hanoi, Vietnam**—The "Paris of Asia" boasts amazing food, history, and landscapes, without the fanny-pack follies of Thailand.

8. **Vancouver, British Columbia**—That's right, I'm talking about Canada. The lovely city of Vancouver is one of the greenest places in North America.

9. **Dubrovnik, Croatia**—The confluence of Mediterranean, Middle Eastern, and Eastern European cultures couldn't be a better setting for some of the most pristine beaches you will ever see.

10. **Buenos Aires, Argentina**—Argentina is heaven for meat-eaters and wine-drinkers. The countryside is exquisite, and there are endless places to explore.

OPPOSITE: If you can't physically travel for whatever reasons, be sure to expand your horizons mentally through books and films.

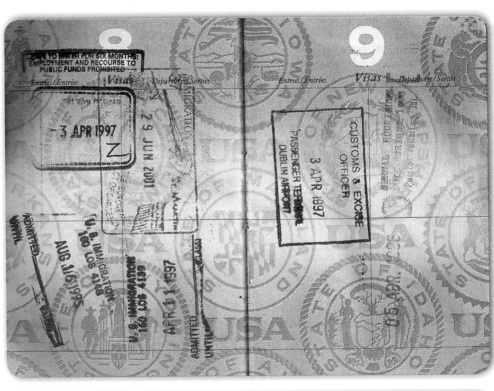

PARADISE IS
WHERE YOU
FIND IT.

Badasses on Wheels

Even though we've come a long way, baby, as the old pseudofemi-nist Virginia Slims cigarette ads used to say, I still think that when it comes to buying a car, most women try to make sure they bring a guy along with them to help them check out the merchandise and wheel and deal for them at the local dealerships and used car lots.

Not my friends.

They send me to do the negotiating. Why? Because I'm a badass! Having become a master at living the badass lifestyle, I find that the most important thing when negotiating for a car—or for anything, for that matter—is being willing to walk away! So burn this motto into your badass brain: "The one who cares the least wins."

I draw a very hard line when negotiating in everything, and when it comes to a car, I make sure I know what my budget is. Then I try to come in a good bit under it. Never, under any circumstances, will I ever—not for anything— go over. If the salesperson isn't willing to budge, I leave.

"THE ONE WHO CARES THE LEAST WINS."

Remember, an authentic badass gal is *always* ready and willing to walk away from a bad deal. It could be a marriage proposal or a job offer or a "final" price on the car of your dreams. A badass woman never, ever has an issue with saying *sayonara*—especially since by doing so, she knows she can very often end up with a much sweeter deal. Or, at the very least, she knows and respects her boundaries.

Try it sometime. Just for practice. Especially these days, with the economy in the Dumpster.

Practice your badass skills of negotiation by window-shopping at a nearby car dealership. Look your best. Go alone. Pick out your favorite air-conditioned chariot and swoon. Take it for a test drive. Flirt with the salesperson. When they come back to you with a selling price, put on your best actress hat and express shock and horror! Turn on your heel and hightail it out of the showroom, saying you know you can get it for a much better price down the road. Walk out.

Count to ten.

Then turn around. I can almost guarantee the salesperson will be standing right there, pen in hand, saying they're sure they can "do a little better" for you. Smile and say thanks, but you gotta run. Now you know how to negotiate for yourself. It's part of living the badass lifestyle, class 101.

A BADASS WOMAN NEVER, EVER HAS AN ISSUE WITH SAYING SAYONARA— ESPECIALLY SINCE BY DOING SO, SHE KNOWS SHE CAN VERY OFTEN END UP WITH A MUCH SWEETER DEAL.

Note that in all things badass, it's also very important to have done your research before you go in for the kill. Use the Internet. You can look at all the different dealerships and the deals they are offering. Go in armed with as much information as you can.

Now, when it comes to buying a used car, the badass gal's strategy for negotiating supremacy is just a tad bit different. Primarily, you need to actually *know* cars. If automotive knowledge is not your particular specialty, and you don't have a good friend whose it is, then get your mechanic to go along with you. That's called a badass gal's ace in the hole.

HOW A BADASS GETS OUT OF A TICKET

We are speeding along, listening to music, trying to get where we are going as quickly as possible, and oops! What's that sound? Sirens . . . crap. I have found that honesty is the best policy in this situation. I have often looked at a cop and just flat-out told the truth; here's how it went for me . . .

Cop: Do you have any idea why I pulled you over?

Me: Um, yeah. Probably because I was speeding.

Cop: Do you know how fast you were going?

Me: Not exactly, but I am sure I was over the speed limit.

Cop: You were going sixty in a fifty.

Me: Yep, sounds about right. I'm sorry; my head is up my ass today. I have a million things to do and although I was speeding, I was driving carefully.

Cop: Okay, well, I can let you go with a warning—but slow down!

Me: Thank you so much, officer.

There is an alternate ending, which goes like this . . .

Cop: I don't care why you were speeding; you are endangering others' lives. Driver's license and registration, please.

Me: (Crap.) Okay.

Here's the thing: police officers have a very hard job, and are constantly putting themselves in danger on the front lines, and I believe they deserve an enormous amount of respect. They are simply doing their jobs and keeping us safe, so please try to be kind and respectful.

That being said, here are a few excuses you can try:

1. I just started my period and have to get home for a tampon now!

2. I have diarrhea and can't hold it.

3. My husband (or boyfriend) is to blame.

4. I am an idiot—so sorry.

As a professional actress I recommend having a little fun while you're at it. I like to make "oh, no" faces or look unsure about this car or that—to throw the seller off a bit. Again, living the badass gal lifestyle means that you're always looking for that extra edge.

That is my way of doing it. My grandmother and mother do it differently—with just as good results. They play the Southern card of charm and needing a man's help. Works for them every time!

Hey, being a badass gal does not mean we can't fall back on our feminine wiles. As I've said all along, a badass woman works it. She owns it. And the it that she owns and works is her badass self!

ABOVE: A badass maps out her journey and then makes it happen.

The Importance of Continuing Your Education

I don't care if you dropped out of school in junior high, high school, whatever—in order to live the lifestyle of an authentic badass, all that matters now is that you educate yourself to be a well-informed human being who can talk about myriad subjects with knowledge and authority.

We all know those people at cocktail parties or what have you who read something about this or that on the Internet or watched a show about this or that on the Discovery or History Channel or read about this or that novel or memoir in the review section of the newspaper, and then repeat the sound bites with confidence, all to appear smart. And yet if you ask them for even the tiniest little extra detail, they are often stumped.

Hello! If you aspire to be an authentic badass gal, DO NOT BE THAT PERSON!

If you see something on television or read about it and it fascinates you enough that you actually want to bring it up in conversation, why not take it a step further and actually do more research so you can expand on it and learn something? I think a badass is *always* learning, constantly trying to improve herself. We pride ourselves on knowing that education is hugely important. We now have at our fingertips the ability to look up any piece of information there is, and read views on it from all different standpoints.

Don't just read one article and take it as the gospel truth; read everything on the subject you can find! Discover your own view on the subject and, while you are at it, look up what else is going on in the world. Don't isolate your mind to only what is going on in your own town or city or country or social life. We live in a world that is constantly in flux, with a whole host of good and bad events that you might just find fascinating.

Authentic badasses love to learn. We love to be one of the smart people in the room, though we never **AUTHENTIC BADASSES** flaunt it. We enjoy having earned the **LOVE TO LEARN.** reputation of being someone of high intelligence, of being a cultured human being. We don't act all snooty about it. We don't need to. We're the real deal. We've got nothing to prove.

Who knows? Now that you're learning to live the lifestyle of an authentic badass, you just might be inspired to take a more hands-on approach and attitude toward this incredible planet we are lucky enough to reside on. There are amazing books out there, like the Oxford series, that will give you a great crash course on American and European history, politics of the world, and so on. There are tons of articles that will teach you about our planet, going green, global warming—all sorts of current issues.

Being observant isn't enough to give you that badass gal edge that all B.A.s have in spades. You've got to take it upon yourself to educate yourself about absolutely everything under the sun. You don't need to become an expert on everything, but you must know what's going on in your world and in your life. Badasses pay attention! They learn from everything and everyone. They keep their eye on the ball at all times. They observe. They study. They read newspapers (especially the world and local news sections). They keep up on current events. They read books. They research. They rummage. They retain details and facts and aspects of everything they encounter. They soak up their surroundings like a sponge. They become the mistress of their own universe. They are not only book smart, but also street-smart beyond compare.

ABOVE: My great love for animals makes me comfortable around them all. . . . Well, almost all!

OVERLEAF: Not only do I love to travel to faraway places, I like to fly myself there. I've been working on getting my pilot's license.

Badasses' Pets

The most badass of all things to have by your side? You guessed it—a pup. But this applies only if you truly love dogs. Because anyone who would get a dog, or any pet for that matter, to use as a fashion accessory is a pathetic person and not badass in the least.

I also love having horses in my life. The sport of horseback riding combined with the emotional connection I have with my horses is unparalleled. There is nothing Cabbage Patch about a badass girl and her pony.

Top 10 Badass Dog Breeds

These dogs are smart, loyal, and stylish. Just like their owners, they also have killer instincts.

1. **German shepherd**

2. **Mastiff**

3. **Golden retriever**

4. **Standard poodle**

5. **Papillon**

6. **Rottweiler**

7. **Australian shepherd**

8. **Labrador retriever**

9. **Border collie**

10. **Australian cattle dog**

OPPOSITE: Riding my horse, Picasso, gets me outdoors and active.

TOP 10 RULES TO LIVING THE BADASS LIFESTYLE

1. BE TRUE TO YOURSELF.

2. BE HONEST WITH YOURSELF AND OTHERS.

3. BE BRAVE.

4. BE ADVENTUROUS.

5. BE KIND.

6. BE BOLD.

7. BE WELL-INFORMED AND WELL-EDUCATED.

8. BE SELF-MOTIVATED.

9. BE JUST A LITTLE BIT "OFF."

10. BE CONFIDENT!

Badasses Are All In

Embrace your zaniness. All the badass gals I have ever admired had some kind of wacky craziness about them. It made them unique. They also all had a different way of looking at things in life. They never saw things in black and white. Train your own eye to look at situations in a different way.

Badass gals eat! But we also exercise. We are never bulimic. You can't be a badass femme fatale if you're dying from starvation. By educating yourself, and by knowing yourself, you are prepared to nourish yourself in a healthy

EMBRACE YOUR ZANINESS.

and pleasurable way. Just be discerning. Don't hitch your wagon to something just because it's trendy. The secret is to be truly invested in what you are campaigning for or talking to others about. There is nothing sexier than a woman with knowledge and a sharp mind. Throw in a lot of confidence, self-esteem, personal style, authenticity, integrity, honesty, strong personal beliefs, and family values, and you've got what it takes to be a real badass.

TAKE THE BADASS PLEDGE!

PUT YOUR HAND OVER YOUR HEART
AND REPEAT THE FOLLOWING WORDS:

I, [say your name here], being of sound mind and body, do solemnly swear to always strive to live up to the best of my badass potential—in every way, every day—or to exhaust myself trying. So help me, God. (Now click your heels and spin around twice.)

Voilà! You are now an honorary badass.

(You'll get your "authentic credentials" when you start walking the walk . . . or better yet, running the run!)

Acknowledgments

As this is my first book, there are so many people to thank.

First and foremost, I thank God for blessing me with so much.

Thank you to my parents, who have stood by me and shown me what humility, love, grace, strength, compassion, and respect are. You believed in me at all times and have been my rock through thick and thin. I know I tell you every day how much I love you both, but it never seems enough to me. Thank you for your integrity, your honesty, your trust, your respect, and your love.

To my brother Sean, Thanne, and their seven amazing kids. Your family is extraordinary beyond words, special, smart . . . the list goes on, and that is a tribute to both of your parenting skills. Sean, thank you for being a strong shoulder to lean on and for all the challenges you set in front of me from the time I was born. To have a brother like you means to constantly strive to catch up, to be as smart, grounded, and ambitious. You along with Mom and Dad helped me become who I am today. Thank you. I love you.

My Adam Kaller. You have stood by me for more than fourteen years and are my constant. You never wavered in your support of me but were always honest with me regardless of my wanting to hear it or not. Your belief in me has always set me on the right track and means the world to me. I rely on you, I admire you, I respect you, and I love you. You, sir, are the real deal and a true badass. Thank you for being in my life. (And, Dana, thank you for sharing him with me and being a kick-ass woman.)

Leslie Sloane, what has it been, fifteen years? You have never wavered, not once, and I appreciate you more than I could ever express. You are a lioness who protects her "young" while giving them support and love. You are my friend, who I have the greatest respect for and cherish. Your strength in your own life has been an inspiration to me, and I can say this with one hundred percent commitment: You are a *badass*, my friend, and one I have learned a great deal from. My favorite time with you: Corey and Bailey are asleep, and we have our late-night girl chats. Love you.

Granny Wright and Papa Wright, the two original badasses. It all starts with you two and the love, dedication, and values with which you raised your family. Thank you for my mom, thank you for your love, and thank you for being you. Papa rest in peace; I love you. Granny, you are one true badass—see you soon in Mississippi; I love you.

Dr. Richard Gold, you make my dad laugh, you have kept him safe with your dedication, skill, and love, and, oh, you have the best bedside manner I have ever seen. Thank you for everything you do for my family and for never giving up. We love you.

Dr. Patrick Lyden, your confidence, skill, and knowledge make you a wonder. Thank you for being part of the team and helping my dad through this last difficult stroke and for your continued care of him.

Dr. Neil Buchbinder, you have saved my dad's life countless times, and for that I am forever grateful. Your silent, confident strength exudes out of you and puts the patients and families who you tend to at ease. You have touched my dad's heart and therefore mine. Thank you.

Dr. Stuart Friedman, Dr. Michael Bush, Doris Holmes, Dr. Jana Baumgarten, her rehab staff, and everyone at Cedars-Sinai Medical Center, thank you all for saving and caring for my father. I could not ask for a nicer, more attentive, more considerate group of people looking after my dad. You are all wonderful and I appreciate everything you have done and continue to do.

Dr. Sarah Song and the amazing ER staff at UCLA, thank you for the speed and efficiency you displayed on Christmas 2009. You guys didn't mess around and took care of my dad in an extremely thorough way, helping to pave the way for his recovery.

All my friends (you know who you are), thank you! An essential part of being a badass is having badass friends, and that I do. I love you guys.

Rosy Ngo and everyone at Clarkson Potter, thank you for bearing with me during this process and respecting my opinion. Rosy, it was tough at times, but having a badass editor like you helped a ton. Thank you.

Last but certainly not least . . .

Kurt, I finally found my badass partner. With an eye that is unique and exceptional, you find beauty where others can't. Your work moves me, your intelligence intrigues me, your humor beguiles me, your creativity captivates me, and your love feeds me. There is not one thing I would change about our journey because of where we are and what we have learned. You are my best friend and my soul mate. I love you.

Index